MONOGRAPHS ON
APPLIED PROBABILITY AND STATISTICS

═══

General Editor: MAURICE BARTLETT

STOCHASTIC PROCESSES

D1635180

Stochastic Processes

PROBLEMS AND SOLUTIONS

L. TAKÁCS D.Sc.

Professor of Mathematics
Case Western Reserve University

Translated by

P. ZÁDOR

LONDON

CHAPMAN AND HALL

First published 1960

*First published as a Science Paperback 1966 by
Chapman and Hall Ltd
11 New Fetter Lane, London, EC4P 4EE
Reprinted twice
Reprinted 1978*

ISBN 0 412 20340 5

*Printed in Great Britain by
J. W. Arrowsmith Ltd, Bristol BS3 2NT*

*Distributed in the U.S.A. by
Halsted Press, a Division of
John Wiley & Sons, Inc.,
New York*

TO MY MOTHER

CONTENTS

GENERAL EDITOR'S PREFACE

It is not so very long ago that up-to-date text-books on statistics were almost non-existent. In the last few decades this deficiency has largely been remedied, but in order to cope with a broad and rapidly expanding subject many of these books have been fairly big and expensive. The success of Methuen's existing series of monographs, in physics or in biology, for example, stresses the value of short inexpensive treatments to which a student can turn for an introduction to, or a revision of, specialised topics.

In this new Methuen series the still-growing importance of probability theory in its applied aspects has been recognised by coupling together Probability and Statistics; and included in the series are some of the newer applications of probability theory to stochastic models in various fields, storage and service problems, 'Monte Carlo' techniques, etc., as well as monographs on particular statistical topics.

M. S. BARTLETT

AUTHOR'S PREFACE

The theory of stochastic processes has developed in the last three decades. Its field of application is constantly expanding and at present it is being applied in nearly every branch of science. So far several books have been written on the mathematical theory of stochastic processes. The nature of this book is different because it is primarily a collection of problems and their solutions, and is intended for readers who are already familiar with probability theory. Its aim is to summarise the fundamental notions and theorems of stochastic processes. The proofs of the theorems are generally omitted or only a brief outline is given. The main body of the book comprises a series of systematically arranged problems, the solutions of which may help the reader to understand the theory and the methods of stochastic processes. The book contains all the basic theorems by which the problems can be solved. In addition, a complete solution is given for each problem.

The scope of this book extends over the theory of Markov chains, Markov processes, stationary stochastic processes, recurrent processes and secondary stochastic processes. The problems are taken from the field of natural sciences, engineering and industry. Their solutions contain several mathematical models which can be applied in investigating empirical processes in these fields.

The book is a revised version of an earlier text which appeared in Hungarian as part of a problem book on probability theory† and I should like to thank Mr P. Zádor for translating it from the Hungarian original.

LAJOS TAKÁCS

New York
December 1959

† P. Medgyessy and L. Takács: *Valószinűségszámitás.* Tankönyvkiadó, Budapest, 1957.

INTRODUCTION

The theory of stochastic processes plays an important role in the investigation of random phenomena depending on time. The first results in this direction were concerned with the investigation of Brownian-motion, telephone traffic and shot-noise of electronic tubes [*A. Einstein* (1905), *M. Smoluchowski* (1906), *L. Bachelier* (1912), *A. K. Erlang* (1918), *W. Schottky* (1918)]. The foundation of the mathematical theory of stochastic processes was given by *A. N. Kolmogorov* (1931). Since that time the theory and applications of stochastic processes have shown a constant development. The mathematical theory of stochastic processes is treated in *J. L. Doob's* book (1953). The applications of stochastic processes are treated in several books; for example, *A. Blanc-Lapierre* and *R. Fortet* (1953), *M. S. Bartlett* (1955); and in numerous scientific publications, some of which are listed in the bibliography.

Definition of a stochastic process
An arbitrary infinite family of real random variables $\{\xi_t, t \in T\}$ *is called a stochastic process.*

If T is a denumerably infinite sequence then $\{\xi_t\}$ is called a *stochastic process with discrete parameter* or a *stochastic sequence*. If T is a finite or infinite interval, then $\{\xi_t\}$ is called a *stochastic process with continuous parameter* or, briefly, a *stochastic process*.

In most applications we can interpret t as the time parameter. Then T is the time interval involved and ξ_t is the observation at time t.

The *fundamental theorem* of stochastic processes was proved by *A. N. Kolmogorov* (1933).

If the distribution functions $F_{t_1, t_2, \ldots, t_n}(x_1, x_2, \ldots, x_n)$ *are given for all finite* n $(n = 1, 2, \ldots)$ *and for all sets of values* $(t_1, t_2, \ldots, t_n)$ *belonging to* T, *and if these distribution functions are compatible, then*

1

there exists a probability space $(\Omega, \mathfrak{B}, \mathbf{P})$ [Ω is the set of elementary events, $\mathfrak{B}$ is a Borel field of certain subsets of Ω, i.e. the set of random events, and $\mathbf{P}\{A\}$ is the probability measure defined for the random events $A \in \mathfrak{B}$] and a family of random variables $\{\xi_t, t \in T\}$ defined on Ω for which $\mathbf{P}\{\xi_{t_1} \le x_1, \ldots, \xi_{t_n} \le x_n\}$ is equal to the prescribed distribution function for every n $(n = 1, 2, \ldots)$ and every $(t_1, \ldots, t_n) \in T$.

The present book contains only the elements of the theory of stochastic processes of the most important types. Thus we shall consider Markov chains, Markov processes, stationary stochastic sequences, stationary stochastic processes, recurrent stochastic processes and secondary stochastic processes generated by an underlying stochastic process.

Roughly speaking, Markov processes (chains) are stochastic processes (sequences) without after-effect, that is, such processes for which the knowledge of the present state uniquely determines its future stochastic behaviour, and this behaviour does not depend on the past of the process. A stationary stochastic process (or sequence) is one whose distributions are invariant under the translation of the time. The recurrent (or regenerative) stochastic processes are characterised by the existence of such random points (regeneration points or Markov points), after whose occurrence the past of the process does not bear any influence on its future stochastic behaviour. The secondary stochastic processes are those which are generated by a simple basic stochastic process.

In the present book, besides discussing theoretical questions, we shall set problems and give their solutions. The most important fundamental notions and theorems are treated in the theory sections. In general we omit the proofs or only sketch their outlines. The theory is followed by problems for solution. The problems originate from theoretical physics, experimental physics, engineering and industry. In several cases we point out the special applications. The solutions are contained in a separate chapter. All problems can be solved by using the listed theorems only, though in many cases this requires an involved reasoning and lengthy calculation.

Theorems in Chapters 1 and 2 are available in several text-books; most of the results contained in Chapter 3 can be found in scientific papers only. Most of the problems given here are simplified versions of problems treated in recent papers. Therefore, we include several papers in addition to the books in the bibliography from which the interested reader can learn further details of the subject.

CHAPTER 1

MARKOV CHAINS

<hr>

1. The definition of a Markov chain. We can introduce the notion of Markov chains in the simplest way by generalising the notion of independent trials. Let us consider a sequence of consecutive trials. Let $E_1, E_2, \ldots, E_j, \ldots$ be a complete system of events (a mutually exclusive and exhaustive system of events). The number of events may be finite or infinite. Let us consider the outcome of each trial from the point of view of the occurrence of the events E_j ($j = 1, 2, \ldots$) and define the random variables ξ_n ($n = 0, 1, 2, \ldots$) as follows, $\xi_n = j$ if E_j is the outcome of the n-th trial.

When the trials are independent we have

$$\mathbf{P}\{\xi_n = j \mid \xi_0 = i_0, \xi_1 = i_1, \ldots, \xi_{n-1} = i_{n-1}\} = \mathbf{P}\{\xi_n = j\}$$

for all n and for all possible values of the random variables in question.

We arrive at the notion of Markov chains if we assume more generally that the outcome of each new trial depends on the outcome of the directly preceding one but is independent of the outcomes of all former trials. Accordingly we define the notion of Markov chains as follows:

We say that consecutive trials or the associated random variables $\{\xi_n\}$ form a Markov chain if for all n ($n = 1, 2, \ldots$) and for all possible values of the random variables ξ_n ($n = 0, 1, \ldots$)

$$(1) \quad \mathbf{P}\{\xi_n = j \mid \xi_0 = i_0, \xi_1 = i_1, \ldots, \xi_{n-1} = i_{n-1}\}$$
$$= \mathbf{P}\{\xi_n = j \mid \xi_{n-1} = i_{n-1}\}$$

holds.

We speak about a *Markov chain of order r* if in a sequence of trials the outcome of each trial depends on the outcomes of the r directly preceding trials and depends only on these. Accordingly the sequence of random variables $\{\xi_n\}$ forms a Markov chain of order r if, given a fixed r, for all n and for all possible values of the variables, ξ_n $(n = 0, 1, 2, \ldots)$, it is true that

$$\mathbf{P}\{\xi_n = j \mid \xi_0 = i_0, \xi_1 = i_1, \ldots, \xi_{n-1} = i_{n-1}\}$$
$$= \mathbf{P}\{\xi_n = j \mid \xi_{n-r} = i_{n-r}, \ldots, \xi_{n-1} = i_{n-1}\}.$$

Thus we can regard the first definition as the definition of a Markov chain of first order; in what follows we shall deal only with Markov chains of first order without mentioning this again.

Bearing in mind the physical applications, we use the following terminology with regard to Markov chains: we call the events E_j $(j = 1, 2, \ldots)$ the *states of the system*. The probability distribution $\mathbf{P}\{\xi_0 = j\} = P_j(0)$ $(j = 1, 2, \ldots)$ of the random variable ξ_0 is called the *initial distribution*, and the conditional probabilities $\mathbf{P}\{\xi_n = j \mid \xi_{n-1} = i\}$ are called *transition probabilities*. Furthermore, if $\xi_{n-1} = i$ and $\xi_n = j$, then we say that the system made *a transition $E_i \longrightarrow E_j$ at the n-th step*.

If we know the initial distribution and transition probabilities of a Markov chain, we can uniquely determine the probability distribution of each random variable ξ_n $(n = 1, 2, \ldots)$.

It is an important problem to investigate whether there exists a limiting distribution of the random variables ξ_n when $n \longrightarrow \infty$, and if it does how it can be determined.

The homogeneous Markov chains form an important special case of Markov chains. Their characteristic property is that the transition probabilities $\mathbf{P}\{\xi_n = j \mid \xi_{n-1} = i\}$ are independent of n; that is, we can write

$$\mathbf{P}\{\xi_n = j \mid \xi_{n-1} = i\} = p_{ij}.$$

If the transition probabilities depend on n we speak of *inhomogeneous Markov chains*. In what follows we shall deal only with homogeneous Markov chains of the first order.

Remark: *A. A. Markov* (1856–1922), Russian mathematician, arrived at the notion of Markov chains when he examined the alternation of vowels and consonants in Pushkin's poem 'Onegin'. Since then *A. A. Markov, V. I. Romanovsky, A. N. Kolmogorov, W. Doeblin, J. L. Doob, W. Feller, K. L. Chung* and others have proved several new theorems in this field. Finally we mention the books of *V. I. Romanovsky* and *T. A. Sarymsakov*, and furthermore that of *W. Feller* in which Chapters 15 and 16 treat the theory of Markov chains.

2. Transition and absolute probabilities. Consider a homogeneous Markov chain of first order with transition probabilities

(2) $\qquad p_{ij} = \mathbf{P}\{\xi_n = j \mid \xi_{n-1} = i\}, \qquad (i, j = 1, 2, \ldots).$

Furthermore, write $\mathbf{P}\{\xi_n = j\} = P_j(n)$.

It obviously holds that

$$\sum_{j=1}^{\infty} p_{ij} = 1, \qquad (i = 1, 2, \ldots) \quad \text{and} \quad p_{ij} \geq 0.$$

The transition probabilities p_{ij} can be arranged in the following matrix form

(3) $\qquad \pi = \left\| \begin{matrix} p_{11} & p_{12} & p_{13} & \cdots \\ p_{21} & p_{22} & p_{23} & \cdots \\ p_{31} & p_{32} & p_{33} & \cdots \\ \cdot & \cdot & \cdot & \cdots \\ \cdot & \cdot & \cdot & \cdots \end{matrix} \right\|.$

This is the so-called *matrix of transition probabilities*. The matrix π is square, its elements are non-negative and the row sums are 1. A matrix of this type is called a *stochastic matrix*.

The stochastic behaviour of a Markov chain is uniquely determined if the matrix π and the initial distribution $\{P_j(0)\}$ are specified.

In order to determine the distribution $\{P_j(n)\}$ we introduce the notion of *n-step transition probabilities*. These are defined as follows:

(4) $\qquad p_{ij}^{(n)} = \mathbf{P}\{\xi_{m+n} = j \mid \xi_m = i\}.$

It is easily seen that in the case of a homogeneous Markov chain these conditional probabilities do not depend on m.

Making use of the total probability theorem we can determine the *absolute probabilities* $P_j(n)$ as follows:

(5) $\qquad P_j(n) = \sum_i P_i(0) p_{ij}^{(n)}.$

The calculation of the *n-step* probabilities $p_{ij}^{(n)}$ can be reduced to the knowledge of the transition probabilities p_{ij}. For, by the total probability theorem we can write the following recurrence formula:

$$(6) \qquad p_{ik}^{(n)} = \sum_j p_{ij} p_{jk}^{(n-1)}, \qquad (n = 1, 2, \ldots),$$

where $p_{jk}^{(0)} = \delta_{jk}$ (Kronecker symbol, $\delta_{jk} = 0$ if $j \neq k$ and $\delta_{jk} = 1$ if $j = k$) and in particular $p_{jk}^{(1)} = p_{jk}$. (Cf. Problem 2.)

If we arrange the transition probabilities $p_{ij}^{(n)}$ in matrix form, then this matrix will be the n-th power of π, that is π^n. This can be deduced by induction on the basis of the rule of matrix multiplication using the recurrence formula (6).

3. Determination of the higher transition probabilities. The recurrence formula (6) always determines $p_{ik}^{(n)}$; however, special methods are often more expedient. In what follows we shall become acquainted with the matrix theoretical method for calculating the transition probabilities $p_{ik}^{(n)}$.

Let the number of states of a Markov chain be m (finite). First we assume that the eigenvalues of the transition probability matrix $\pi = \| p_{ik} \|$ $(i, k = 1, 2, \ldots, m)$, that is the roots of equation $| \pi - \lambda I | = 0$, are simple.[†] We denote by x_j and y_j' the left and right eigenvectors of π belonging to the eigenvalue $\lambda = \lambda_j$ (x_j and y_j are column vectors), that is, the solutions of the equations $\pi x_j = \lambda_j x_j$ and $y_j' \pi = \lambda_j y_j'$ respectively. We remark that the equations $\pi x = \lambda x$ and $y'\pi = \lambda y'$ have solutions x and y other than zero if and only if λ is an eigenvalue of the matrix π. If $j \neq k$ we have $y_j' x_k = 0$ and by choosing a suitable multiplicative factor we can achieve $y_j' x_j = 1$ $(j = 1, 2, \ldots, m)$. With this choice

$$H = \| x_1, x_2, \ldots, x_m \| \quad \text{and} \quad H^{-1} = \begin{Vmatrix} y_1' \\ y_2' \\ \cdot \\ \cdot \\ \cdot \\ y_m' \end{Vmatrix}$$

[†] $I = \| \delta_{ik} \|$ $(i, k = 1, 2, \ldots, m)$ denotes the unit matrix. A' is the transposed matrix of A (that is, a matrix which is obtained by interchanging the rows and columns of A). The inverse of A is A^{-1}. The determinant of a square matrix A will be denoted by $| A |$.

are inverse matrices, and by means of these matrices we can write

$$(7) \qquad \pi = H\Lambda H^{-1}$$

where Λ is a diagonal matrix the elements of which are the eigenvalues of π; that is

$$\Lambda = \begin{Vmatrix} \lambda_1 & 0 & \dots & 0 \\ 0 & \lambda_2 & \dots & 0 \\ \cdot & \cdot & \dots & \cdot \\ 0 & 0 & \dots & \lambda_m \end{Vmatrix}.$$

Now by means of (7) it is easily seen that

$$(8) \qquad \pi^n = H\Lambda^n H^{-1},$$

where

$$\Lambda^n = \begin{Vmatrix} \lambda_1^n & 0 & \dots & 0 \\ 0 & \lambda_2^n & \dots & 0 \\ \cdot & \cdot & \dots & \cdot \\ 0 & 0 & \dots & \lambda_m^n \end{Vmatrix}.$$

Using formula (8), the transition probabilities $p_{ik}^{(n)}$ can be determined easily. If the eigenvectors $\mathbf{x}_j$ and $\mathbf{y}_j$ are arbitrarily chosen, then we can write

$$(9) \qquad \pi^n = \sum_{j=1}^{m} C_j \lambda_j^n \mathbf{x}_j \mathbf{y}_j'$$

where $C_j = 1/\mathbf{y}_j' \mathbf{x}_j$. Accordingly, if

$$\mathbf{x}_j = \begin{Vmatrix} \alpha_{1j} \\ \alpha_{2j} \\ \cdot \\ \cdot \\ \cdot \\ \alpha_{mj} \end{Vmatrix} \quad \text{and} \quad \mathbf{y}_j = \begin{Vmatrix} \beta_{j_1} \\ \beta_{j_2} \\ \cdot \\ \cdot \\ \cdot \\ \beta_{jm} \end{Vmatrix},$$

then

$$(10) \qquad p_{ik}^{(n)} = \sum_{j=1}^{m} C_j \lambda_j^m \alpha_{ij} \beta_{jk},$$

where

$$(11) \qquad C_j = 1 \Big/ \sum_{\nu=1}^{m} \beta_{j\nu} \alpha_{\nu j}.$$

By (9) we have

$$(12) \qquad \pi^n = \sum_{j=1}^{m} \lambda_j^n \mathbf{A}_j,$$

where $\mathbf{A}_1, \mathbf{A}_2, \ldots, \mathbf{A}_m$ are fixed matrices independent of n. If we introduce the Lagrange interpolation polynomials

$$L_j(z) = \prod_{\substack{v=1 \\ v \neq j}}^{n} \left(\frac{z - \lambda_v}{\lambda_j - \lambda_v} \right)$$

then we have

$$\mathbf{A}_j = L_j(\pi).$$

The matrices $\mathbf{A}_j \ (j = 1, 2, \ldots, m)$ satisfy the relations

$$\sum_{j=1}^{m} \mathbf{A}_j = \mathbf{I} \quad \text{and} \quad \mathbf{A}_j\mathbf{A}_k = \begin{array}{ll} \mathbf{A}_k & \text{if} \quad j = k \\ 0 & \text{if} \quad j \neq k. \end{array}$$

If the matrix π has also multiple eigenvalues, then we shall have the following canonical representation. Suppose the matrix π has elementary divisors $(\lambda - \lambda_1)^{\rho_1}, (\lambda - \lambda_2)^{\rho_2}, \ldots, (\lambda - \lambda_p)^{\rho_p}$, where $\rho_1 + \rho_2 + \ldots + \rho_p = m$ (the eigenvalues $\lambda_1, \lambda_2, \ldots, \lambda_p$ are not necessarily different). In this case there exists a non-singular matrix $\mathbf{H}$ such that

$$(13) \qquad \pi = \mathbf{H}\mathbf{\Lambda}\mathbf{H}^{-1},$$

where the partitioned matrix $\mathbf{\Lambda}$ is of the form

$$\mathbf{\Lambda} = \left\| \begin{array}{ccccc} \mathbf{I}_{\rho_1}(\lambda_1) & 0 & 0 & \ldots & 0 \\ 0 & \mathbf{I}_{\rho_2}(\lambda_2) & 0 & \ldots & 0 \\ \cdot & & \cdot & \ldots & \cdot \\ 0 & 0 & 0 & \ldots & \mathbf{I}_{\rho_p}(\lambda_p) \end{array} \right\|,$$

and here

$$\mathbf{I}_\rho(\lambda) = \left\| \begin{array}{cccccc} \lambda & 1 & 0 & \ldots & 0 & 0 \\ 0 & \lambda & 1 & \ldots & 0 & 0 \\ \cdot & \cdot & \cdot & \ldots & \cdot & \cdot \\ 0 & 0 & 0 & \ldots & \lambda & 1 \\ 0 & 0 & 0 & \ldots & 0 & \lambda \end{array} \right\|.$$

particular, $\mathbf{I}_1(\lambda) = \lambda$.

Now according to (13) we have

(14) $$\pi^n = H\Lambda^n H^{-1}$$

and

$$\Lambda^n = \begin{Vmatrix} \mathbf{I}_{\rho_1}^n(\lambda_1) & 0 & 0 & \ldots & 0 \\ 0 & \mathbf{I}_{\rho}^n(\lambda_2) & 0 & \ldots & 0 \\ \cdot & \cdot & \cdot & \ldots & \cdot \\ 0 & 0 & 0 & \ldots & \mathbf{I}_{\rho_p}^n(\lambda_p) \end{Vmatrix}.$$

where

$$\mathbf{I}_{\rho}^n(\lambda) = \begin{Vmatrix} \lambda^n & \binom{n}{1}\lambda^{n-1} & \ldots & \binom{n}{\rho-1}\lambda^{n-\rho+1} \\ 0 & \lambda^n & \ldots & \binom{n}{\rho-2}\lambda^{n-\rho+2} \\ 0 & \cdot & \ldots & \cdot \\ 0 & 0 & \ldots & \lambda^n \end{Vmatrix}.$$

By means of (14) we can easily obtain the transition probabilities $p_{ik}^{(n)}$.

Even if the number of states is denumerably infinite we can often successfully apply the matrix-theoretical method to determine the higher transition probabilities $p_{ik}^{(n)}$.

4. Classification of states. We say that the state E_k can be reached from the state E_j if there exists a number $n > 0$ such that $p_{jk}^{(n)} > 0$. A Markov chain is called *irreducible* if every state can be reached from every other state.

We say that a set C of states in a Markov chain is *closed* if it is impossible to move out from any state of C to any state outside C by one-step transitions, that is $p_{jk} = 0$ if $E_j \in C$ and $E_k \notin C$. In this case $p_{jk}^{(n)} = 0$ obviously holds for every n. If a single state E_k forms a closed set, then we call this an *absorbing state*. Then we have $p_{kk} = 1$.

In an irreducible Markov chain the set of all states forms a closed set and no other set is closed.

If we consider only the states of a closed set C, then we have a sub-Markov chain defined on C, and this can be studied independently of the other states.

Let us consider an arbitrary but fixed state E_j. Suppose that the system initially is in state E_j ($\xi_0 = j$). Denote by $f_j^{(n)}$ the probability that the *first return* to E_j occurs at the n-th step. The probabilities $f_j^{(n)}(n = 1, 2, \ldots)$ can be determined by the following recurrence formulae:

$$(15) \qquad p_{jj}^{(n)} = \sum_{m=1}^{n} f_j^{(m)} p_{jj}^{(n-m)}, \qquad (n = 1, 2, \ldots).$$

Equation (15) can be proved by the total probability theorem. The probability that the system *returns at least once* to the state E is

$$(16) \qquad f_j = \sum_{n=1}^{\infty} f_j^{(n)}.$$

If $f_j = 1$, that is the system returns to E_j with probability 1, then we can define the expectation of the number of steps which precede the first return as follows:

$$(17) \qquad \mu_j = \sum_{n=1}^{\infty} n f_j^{(n)};$$

this is called *mean recurrence time*. (If $f_j < 1$, then $\mu_j = \infty$.)

After these introductory remarks we can classify the states of a Markov chain as follows:

A state E_j is *recurrent* if a return to E_j is certain, that is, $f_j = 1$. A state is *transient* if a return to it is uncertain, that is, $f_j < 1$.

Denote by T the set of transient states. The recurrent states can be divided into mutually disjoint closed sets $C_1, C_2, \ldots$ such that from any state of a given set all states of that set and no others can be reached. States in $C_1, C_2, \ldots$ can be reached from states in T, but not conversely.

The state E_j is called *periodic* with period t if a return to E_j can occur only at steps $t, 2t, 3t, \ldots$ and $t > 1$ is the greatest integer with this property. Then $p_{jj}^{(n)} = 0$ whenever n is not divisible by t.

All states of a closed set have the same period. Therefore we can speak of the period of the closed set C. If C is a closed set with period t, then the states of C can be divided into disjoint sub-sets $G_0, G_1, \ldots, G_{t-1}$ in such a way that one-step transition leads always from a state of G_ν into a state of $G_{\nu+1}$ ($G_t = G_0$). If $t = 1$, then we say that the state E_j and the closed set C are *aperiodic* (non-periodic).

The recurrent state E_j is called a *null-state* whenever the mean recurrence time is infinite, that is $f_j = 1$ and $\mu = \infty$.

We say that the recurrent state E_j is *ergodic* if it is not a null-state and is aperiodic, that is if $f_j = 1$, $\mu_j < \infty$ and $t = 1$.

Theorem 1. All states of an irreducible Markov chain belong to the same class: they are either all transient states or all recurrent null-states or all recurrent non-null states. Their periods are always the same.

Remark: A chain with a finite number of states cannot contain a null-state, and cannot consist of transient states only.

5. The limit of the higher transition probabilities. If E_k is a transient or recurrent null-state, then for arbitrary E_j

$$(18) \qquad \lim_{n \to \infty} p_{jk}^{(n)} = 0$$

holds.

Suppose that E_j and E_k are recurrent states and they belong to the same closed set C. If C is aperiodic we have:

$$(19) \qquad \lim_{n \to \infty} p_{jk}^{(n)} = \frac{1}{\mu_k},$$

irrespective of j, if C has a period $t > 1$ and $E_j \in G_\nu$, then

$$(20) \qquad \lim_{n \to \infty} p_{jk}^{(nt+r)} = \begin{cases} t/\mu_k & \text{if } E_k \in G_{\nu+r}, \\ 0 & \text{if } E_k \notin G_{\nu+r}. \end{cases}$$

(Here $G_{\nu'} \equiv G_\nu$ if $\nu' \equiv \nu$ (mod. t).)

It remains still to consider the case when E_j is a transient state ($E_j \in T$) and E_k is a recurrent state. Let E_k belong to the closed set C (that is, $E_k \in C$). If C is aperiodic ($t = 1$), then

$$(21) \qquad \lim_{n \to \infty} p_{jk}^{(n)} = \frac{\pi_j^*}{\mu_k}$$

holds, where π_j^* is the probability that the system starting from E_j

ultimately will reach and stay in the closed set C. The *absorption probabilities* $\pi_j^*(E_j \in T)$ form the minimal non-negative solution of the following system of linear equations:

$$(22) \qquad \pi_j^* = \sum_{E_v \in T} p_{jv} \pi_v^* + \sum_{E_k \in C} p_{jk}, \qquad (E_j \in T).$$

If C has period $t > 1$ the situation becomes more complicated, but it is true in all cases that the limiting probabilities

$$(23) \qquad \lim_{n \to \infty} p_{jk}^{(nt+r)} \qquad (r = 0, 1, \ldots, t - 1)$$

exist and are non-zero for one or more (perhaps for all) values of r.

6. Classification of Markov chains. We have already mentioned that a Markov chain is called *irreducible* if and only if all its states form a closed set and there is no other closed set contained in it.

A Markov chain is called *ergodic* if the probability distributions $\{P_j(n)\}$ always converge to a limiting distribution $\{P_j\}$ which is independent of the initial distribution $\{P_j(0)\}$, that is, when $\lim_{n \to \infty} P_j(n) = P_j \ (j = 1, 2, \ldots)$.

If all states of a Markov chain are ergodic, then the Markov chain is also ergodic.

The probability distribution $\{P_j^*\}$ is a *stationary distribution* of a Markov chain if when we choose it for an initial distribution all the distributions $\{P_j(n)\}$ will coincide with $\{P_j^*\}$.

A Markov chain $\{\xi_n\}$ is said to be *stationary* if the distributions of the random variables $\xi_n \ (n = 0, 1, 2, \ldots)$ are identical, that is, when the initial distribution is stationary.

It is obvious that every stationary distribution of a Markov chain satisfies the following system of linear equations:

$$(24) \qquad P_k^* = \sum_j P_j^* p_{jk}$$

$$(25) \qquad \sum_k P_k^* = 1,$$

and conversely each solution $\{P_k^*\}$ of this system, if it is a probability distribution, is a stationary distribution of the Markov chain.

If the Markov chain is ergodic, then the limiting distribution is a stationary distribution, and there is no other stationary distribution.

7. The limiting distributions of irreducible Markov chains. The limiting distribution $\lim\limits_{n \to \infty} P_j(n) = P_j$ $(j = 1, 2, \ldots)$ can easily be determined when $\lim\limits_{n \to \infty} p_{jk}^{(n)}$ is known. Now we shall deal with the problem of the existence of the limiting distribution $\{P_j\}$. We consider first the aperiodic case.

Theorem 2. Let us assume that the states of an irreducible Markov chain are aperiodic, recurrent non-null states. In this case the limits

$$(26) \qquad \lim_{n \to \infty} P_j(n) = P_j \qquad (j = 1, 2, \ldots)$$

exist and are independent of the initial distribution $\{P_j(0)\}$; furthermore, $\{P_j\}$ is a probability distribution with positive elements, that is

$$(27) \qquad \sum_j P_j = 1 \quad \text{and} \quad P_j > 0.$$

The limiting distribution $\{P_j\}$ can be uniquely determined by solving the following system of linear equations

$$(28) \qquad P_j = \sum_i P_i p_{ij}, \qquad (j = 1, 2, \ldots).$$

Finally the mean recurrence time of the state E_j is $\mu_j = 1/P_j$.

We add that if the states of an irreducible Markov chain are aperiodic and either transient or recurrent-null states, then $\lim\limits_{n \to \infty} P_j(n) = 0$ holds irrespective of the initial distribution $\{P_j(0)\}$.

We now mention two theorems which enable us to decide about the ergodicity of a Markov chain.

According to a theorem of *A. A. Markov* all states of a finite, aperiodic, irreducible Markov chain are ergodic and so we can apply Theorem 2.

The theorem of *F. G. Foster* states that an irreducible and aperiodic Markov chain is ergodic if the following system of linear equations:

$$\sum_i x_i p_{ij} = x \qquad (j = 1, 2, \ldots),$$

has a non-null solution for which

$$\sum_i |x_i| < \infty.$$

It follows from Theorem 2 that if a Markov chain is ergodic, then there exists only one stationary distribution and this is the limiting distribution $\{P_j\}$. If the states of an irreducible and aperiodic Markov chain are transient or null-states, then there is no stationary distribution.

For a physical system we describe the state of statistical equilibrium by a stationary distribution, and the fact that the distributions $\{P_j(n)\}$ converge to the limiting distribution $\{P_j\}$ we interpret as a development towards the state of equilibrium.

Now we consider the case of periodic Markov chains. It follows from what we have said earlier that all states of an irreducible, periodic Markov chain can be divided into sub-sets $G_0, G_1, \ldots G_{t-1}$ in such a way that a one-step transition from a state of G_v leads always to a state of G_{v+1}, $(G_t = G_0)$. Consequently a t-step transition leads necessarily to a state belonging to the same set. If we consider the Markov chain only at times $m = r + nt$ $(n = 0, 1, \ldots)$, then we obtain a new Markov chain with π^t as the transition probability matrix, and in this new Markov chain each G_v forms a closed set. For, the original chain is irreducible and so each state can be reached from every other.

Using the theorems proved for aperiodic Markov chains we can also determine the limiting probabilities for periodic chains.

If a Markov chain possesses only transient or recurrent null-states, then $\lim_{n \to \infty} p_{jk}^{(n)} = 0$ for all j and k and $\lim_{n \to \infty} P_k(n) = 0$ for all k, irrespective of the initial distribution.

Otherwise each state E_k has a finite mean recurrence time μ_k, and if $E_j \in G_v$ we can define an ergodic Markov chain over the states of G_v with transition probabilities $p_{jk}^{(t)}$. Thus the existence of the following limits for $r = 0, 1, 2, \ldots, t - 1$ is guaranteed:

$$\lim_{n \to \infty} p_{jk}^{(nt+r)} = \begin{cases} P_k & \text{if} \quad E_k \in G_{\nu+r} \\ 0 & \text{otherwise} \end{cases}$$

and

$$\mu_k = t/P_k,$$

since t-steps of the original chain correspond to a single-step of the new chain. Hence the limiting distributions $\lim\limits_{n \to \infty} P_k(nt + r)$ can easily be obtained if the initial distribution is known.

The stationary distribution of a Markov chain is now given by $\{P_k/t\}$ and there is no other stationary distribution. The probabilities $P_k^* = P_k/t$ $(k = 1, 2, 3, \ldots)$ can be determined uniquely by solving the system of linear equations (24).

Problems for solution

1. Show that it is true for all Markov chains $\{\xi_n\}$ that

$$\mathbf{P}\{\xi_n = j \mid \xi_{n_1} = i_1, \xi_{n_2} = i_2, \ldots, \xi_{n_s} = i_s\} = \mathbf{P}\{\xi_n = j \mid \xi_{n_s} = i_s\},$$

if $0 \le n_1 < n_2 < \ldots < n_s < n$.

2. Prove (6), i.e. that the equations

$$p_{ik}^{(n)} = \sum_j p_{ij} p_{jk}^{(n-1)} \qquad (n = 1, 2, \ldots)$$

hold.

3. Prove that E_j is recurrent if and only if the sum

$$\sum_{n=1}^{\infty} p_{jj}^{(n)}$$

is divergent and that E_j is transient if and only if this sum is convergent. (*Hint:* Use recurrence formula (15)).

4. Let $F_j(z) = \sum\limits_{n=1}^{\infty} f_j^{(n)} z^n$ and $P_j(z) = \sum\limits_{n=1}^{\infty} p_{jj}^{(n)} z^n$. Prove that if $|z| < 1$ then

$$F_j(z) = \frac{P_j(z)}{1 + P_j(z)}.$$

(*Hint:* Form generating functions in equation (15).)

5. Consider a Markov chain with two states E_1 and E_2, transition probabilities $p_{11} = p_{22} = p$, $p_{12} = p_{21} = q$ (where $0 < p < 1$ and $p + q = 1$) and initial distribution $\mathbf{P}\{\xi_0 = 1\} = \alpha$, $\mathbf{P}\{\xi_0 = 2\} = \beta$ (where $\alpha + \beta = 1$). Determine the n-step transition probabilities $\{p_{jk}^{(n)}\}$, the absolute probabilities $\{P_j(n)\}$ and the limiting probabilities $\{P_j\}$.

6. Determine the conditional probability $\mathbf{P}\{\xi_0 = i \mid \xi_n = j\}$ for a Markov chain $\{\xi_n\}$. (*Hint:* Use Bayes' theorem.)

7. Determine the conditional probability $\mathbf{P}\{\xi_0 = 1 \mid \xi_n = 1\}$ in case of Problem 5.

8. Classify the states of the Markov chains with the following transition probability matrices:

$$\pi = \left\| \begin{array}{ccc} 0 & \frac{1}{2} & \frac{1}{2} \\ \frac{1}{2} & 0 & \frac{1}{2} \\ \frac{1}{2} & \frac{1}{2} & 0 \end{array} \right\|, \quad \pi = \left\| \begin{array}{cccc} 0 & 0 & \frac{1}{2} & \frac{1}{2} \\ 1 & 0 & 0 & 0 \\ 0 & 1 & 0 & 0 \\ 0 & 1 & 0 & 0 \end{array} \right\|, \quad \pi = \left\| \begin{array}{ccccc} \frac{1}{2} & \frac{1}{2} & 0 & 0 & 0 \\ \frac{1}{2} & \frac{1}{2} & 0 & 0 & 0 \\ 0 & 0 & \frac{1}{2} & \frac{1}{2} & 0 \\ 0 & 0 & \frac{1}{2} & \frac{1}{2} & 0 \\ \frac{1}{4} & \frac{1}{4} & 0 & 0 & \frac{1}{2} \end{array} \right\|.$$

9. Consider a Markov chain with a transition probability matrix:

$$\pi = \left\| \begin{array}{ccccc} p_0 & p_1 & p_2 & \cdots & p_{m-1} \\ p_{m-1} & p_0 & p_1 & \cdots & p_{m-2} \\ \cdot & \cdot & \cdot & \cdots & \cdot \\ p_1 & p_2 & p_3 & \cdots & p_0 \end{array} \right\|,$$

where $p_0 + p_1 + \ldots + p_m = 1$ ($p_i \neq 1$). Determine π^m, and prove that
$$\lim_{n \to \infty} P_j(n) = 1/m \qquad (j = 1, 2, \ldots, m).$$

10. N white and N black balls are distributed in two urns in such a way that each contains N balls. We say that the system is in state E_j if the first urn contains j white balls. At each step we draw a ball at random from each urn and put the ball drawn from the first urn back to the second and conversely. Determine the transition probabilities p_{jk} and the limiting distribution $\{P_j\}$.

11. *The Ehrenfest-model of diffusion with a central force.* Consider a Markov chain with states $E_0, E_1, \ldots, E_a$ and transition probabilities $p_{j,j+1} = 1 - j/a$, $p_{j,j-1} = j/a$. Determine the transition probabilities $p_{ik}^{(n)}$ and the stationary distribution $\{P_j^*\}$.

12. *Random walk in the presence of absorbing barriers*. Consider a random walk on the x axis, where there are absorbing barriers at the points $x = 0$ and $x = a$. Let the possible states be $E_0, E_1, \ldots, E_a$, where E_j corresponds to the presence of the particle at point $x = j$. If $1 \leq j \leq a - 1$ the particle can move from E_j either to the state E_{j+1} or to the state E_{j-1}, but if it once reaches the state E_0 or E_a, then it must stay there for ever. Now let us suppose that the transition probabilities are $p_{00} = p_{aa} = 1$ and $p_{j,j+1} = p$, $p_{j,j-1} = q$, where $p + q = 1$. Suppose that the initial state is $E_i(i \neq 0, i \neq a)$, that is $P_i(0) = 1$ and $P_j(0) = 0$ if $j \neq i$. Determine $P_k(n)$ ($k = 1, 2, \ldots, a - 1$) and

$$\lim_{n \to \infty} \mathbf{P}\{\xi_n = 0 \mid \xi_0 = j\} = \pi_j^*.$$

13. *Random walk in the presence of reflecting barriers*. Consider a random walk on the x axis where there are reflecting barriers at the points $x = \frac{1}{2}$ and $x = a + \frac{1}{2}$. Let the possible states of the system be $E_1, E_2, \ldots, E_a$, where E_j corresponds to the presence of the particle at point $x = j$. If $2 \leq j \leq a - 1$ the system can move from E_j either to E_{j-1} or to E_{j+1}, while from E_1 it can go to E_2 or it can stay in E_1, and similarly from E_a it can go to E_{a-1} or it can stay in E_a. Now let the transition probabilities be $p_{11} = q$, $p_{aa} = p$ and $p_{j,j+1} = p$, $p_{j,j-1} = q$, $(p + q = 1)$. Determine the limiting distribution $\{P_j\}$ and the transition probabilities $p_{ik}^{(n)}$.

14. *Problem of waiting-time*. Let us consider a counter with a single server at which customers are arriving in the instants τ_0, $\tau_1, \ldots, \tau_n, \ldots$ Suppose that the inter-arrival times $\tau_n - \tau_{n-1}$ ($n = 1, 2, 3, \ldots$) are identically distributed, independent, positive random variables with distribution function

$$F(x) = \begin{cases} 1 - e^{-\lambda x} & \text{if } x \geq 0, \\ 0 & \text{if } x < 0. \end{cases}$$

If the server is free, then he starts attending an arriving customer immediately. If the server is busy, the newcomers have to wait till those who arrived before them are served. Suppose that the consecutive service-times $\{\chi_n\}$ are independent of each other and of the instants $\{\tau_n\}$, and that they are positive random variables with common distribution functions $H(x)$. Write

$$\alpha = \int_0^\infty x \, dH(x).$$

Consider the successive departures and denote by ξ_n the number of waiting persons after the n-th departure. If $\xi_n = j$, then the system is said to be in state E_j. Determine the limiting probability P_j of the state E_j if $n \to \infty$.

(*Hint:* Obviously we can write for the transition probabilities p_{jk} that $\mathbf{P}\{\xi_n = j \mid \xi_{n-1} = k\} = \pi_{j-k+1}$ if $k \geq 1$ and $j = k - 1,$ $k, \dots$, while $\mathbf{P}\{\xi_n = j \mid \xi_{n-1} = 0\} = \pi_j$ if $j = 0, 1, 2, \dots$, where

$$\pi_j = \int_0^\infty e^{-\lambda x} \frac{(\lambda x)^j}{j!} \, dH(x).)$$

15. *Erlang's formula.* Suppose that at a telephone centre calls are arriving in the instants $\tau_0, \tau_1, \dots, \tau_n, \dots$ Let us suppose that the inter-arrival times $\tau_n - \tau_{n-1}$ $(n = 1, 2, \dots)$ are independent, positive random variables with the same distribution function $F(x)$. Suppose that there are m available channels. If there is a free channel when a call comes in, then a connection is realised; if all channels are busy, then the incoming call is lost. Suppose that the holding times are positive random variables, independent of each other and of the instants $\{\tau_n\}$, and have the same distribution function:

$$H(x) = \begin{cases} 1 - e^{-\mu x} & \text{if } x \geq 0, \\ 0 & \text{if } x < 0. \end{cases}$$

Denote by the random variable ξ_n the number of busy channels at the instant $t = \tau_n - 0$. In this case ξ_n can assume the values $0, 1, \dots, m$, and we say that the possible states of the system are $E_0, E_1, \dots, E_m$ respectively. Determine the limiting distribution $\{P_j\}$.

(*Hint:* We have for the transition probabilities p_{jk} that

$$p_{jk} = \binom{j+1}{k} \int_0^\infty e^{-k\mu x}(1 - e^{-\mu x})^{j+1-k} dF(x),$$

if $j = 0, 1, \dots, m - 1$ and

$$p_{m,k} = p_{m-1,k}.)$$

16. Consider a sequence of random variables $\{\xi_n\}$ defined by the recurrence formula:

$$\xi_n = \begin{cases} \xi_{n-1} - k + \eta_{n-1} & \text{if} \quad \xi_{n-1} \geq k, \\ \xi_{n-1} + \eta_{n-1} & \text{if} \quad \xi_{n-1} < k, \end{cases}$$

where k is a fixed positive integer and the random variables $\{\eta_n\}$ are mutually independent with the distribution

$$\mathbf{P}\{\eta_n = v\} = \binom{m}{v} p^v (1 - p)^{m-v}, \qquad (v = 0, 1, \ldots, m).$$

Show that the sequence of random variables $\{\xi_n\}$ forms a Markov chain and determine the limiting probabilities

$$\lim_{n \to \infty} \mathbf{P}\{\xi_n = j\} = P_j.$$

17. Consider a Markov chain with states $E_0, E_1, E_2, \ldots$ and transition probabilities

$$p_{jk} = e^{-\lambda} \sum_{v=0}^{k} \binom{j}{v} p^v q^{j-v} \frac{\lambda^{k-v}}{(k - v)!},$$

where $p + q = 1$. Show that the limiting distribution $\{P_j\}$ exists and that

$$P_j = e^{-\lambda/q} \frac{(\lambda/q)^j}{j!}, \qquad (j = 0, 1, 2, \ldots).$$

We remark that this Markov chain emerges in connection with problems in statistical mechanics.

18. Let the possible states of a Markov chain be $E_1, E_2, \ldots, E_{2a}$. The system can move from E_j either to E_{j+1} or to E_{j-1}, with probabilities p and q respectively (where $p + q = 1$). ($E_{2a+1} \equiv E_1$ and $E_0 \equiv E_{2a}$). Determine the limit of the transition probabilities $p_{ik}^{(n)}$ and the stationary distribution $\{P_k^*\}$ of the Markov chain.

19. *Chain reaction.* The Markov chain below describes the cascade process in an electron multiplier or the chain reaction which takes place in a nuclear reactor. Let the random variables ξ_n ($n = 0, 1, 2, \ldots$) denote the size of the population of the n-th generation. We suppose that the individuals of the n-th generation are produced by those of the n-1th generation in such a way that each of these can

C

independently of the others give rise to 0, 1, 2, ... successors with probabilities $p_0, p_1, p_2, \ldots$ Then $\{\xi_n\}$ is a homogeneous Markov chain. Let $\xi_0 = j$. Determine π^*, the probability of extinction of the process, that is the probability that at some stage the number of descendants will be 0, provided it was j originally.

20. Consider a Markov chain with states E_1, E_2, E_3, E_4, E_5, and with transition-probability matrix

$$\pi = \begin{Vmatrix} \frac{1}{2} & \frac{1}{4} & 0 & \frac{1}{4} & 0 \\ 0 & 0 & 1 & 0 & 0 \\ 0 & 0 & 0 & 1 & 0 \\ 0 & 0 & 0 & 0 & 1 \\ 0 & 1 & 0 & 0 & 0 \end{Vmatrix}.$$

Determine $\lim_{n \to \infty} p_{13}^{(4n+r)}$ for $r = 0, 1, 2, 3$.

8. Markov chains with continuous state space.

We have supposed up to now that a Markov chain has a finite or denumerably infinite number of states, that is we have supposed that the set of values which can be assumed by the random variables $\xi_0, \xi_1, \ldots, \xi_n, \ldots$ is finite or denumerably infinite (usually the set of integers). Now, more generally we consider the case when the possible states form a continuum. In particular we suppose the range of values assumed by random variables $\{\xi_n\}$ to be equal to the set of real numbers. (As a further generalisation we could assume that the range of values assumed by $\{\xi_n\}$ is an abstract set; however, we shall not deal with this case.)

Consider a sequence of real random variables $\xi_0, \xi_1, \ldots, \xi_n, \ldots$ If

$$(29) \quad \mathbf{P}\{\xi_n \leq x \mid \xi_0 = y_0, \xi_1 = y_1, \ldots, \xi_{n-1} = y_{n-1}\} = \mathbf{P}\{\xi_n \leq x \mid \xi_{n-1} = y_{n-1}\}$$

holds for every n ($n = 1, 2, \ldots$) and for every possible value of the above random variables, then we say that the sequence of random variables $\{\xi_n\}$ forms a Markov chain.

The initial distribution $\mathbf{P}\{\xi_0 \leq x\} = P_0(x)$ and the transition probabilities $\mathbf{P}\{\xi_n \leq x \mid \xi_{n-1} = y\}$ of a Markov chain determine uniquely its stochastic behaviour. In particular, the distribution function $\mathbf{P}\{\xi_n \leq x\} = P_n(x)$ of the random variable ξ_n can also be uniquely determined.

We speak about a *homogeneous Markov chain* when the transition probabilities are independent of n. In this case we can write

(30) $$\mathbf{P}\{\xi_n \leq x \mid \xi_{n-1} = y\} = K(x,y).$$

We say that a Markov chain is *ergodic* when the distributions $\{P_n(x)\}$ tend to a limiting distribution $P(x)$ irrespectively of the initial distribution $P_0(x)$, that is, $\lim_{n \to \infty} P_n(x) = P(x)$ holds for all points of continuity of $P(x)$.

Using the total probability theorem we can write

(31) $$P_n(x) = \int_{-\infty}^{\infty} K(x, y) \, dP_{n-1}(y), \qquad (n = 1, 2, \ldots).$$

Hence if a Markov chain is ergodic, then the limiting distribution $P(x)$ satisfies the integral equation

(32) $$P(x) = \int_{-\infty}^{\infty} K(x, y) \, dP(y)$$

and $P(x)$ is the unique solution of equation (32).

$P^*(x)$ is called a *stationary* distribution if every distribution function $P_n(x)$ is equal to $P^*(x)$ when we choose $P^*(x)$ as an initial distribution.

Every solution $P(x)$ of equation (32) which is a distribution function is also a stationary distribution.

Problems for solution

21. We observe the process of nuclear decay with a particle-counter. The counter tube generates potential impulses $\chi_0, \chi_1, \ldots, \chi_n, \ldots$ on the input resistance of the measuring instrument at moments $\tau_0, \tau_1, \ldots, \tau_n, \ldots$ We suppose that the time intervals $\tau_n - \tau_{n-1}$ $(n = 1, 2, \ldots)$ and the impulses χ_n $(n = 0, 1, 2, \ldots)$ are independent sequences of independent, positive random variables with respective distribution functions $G(x)$ and $H(x)$. The voltage on the input resistance decreases exponentially in time with a time constant RC. Let $\alpha = 1/RC$. Let ξ_n denote the voltage on the input resistance at time $t = \tau_n - 0$. Show that the Markov chain $\{\xi_n\}$ is ergodic, and determine the limiting distribution $P(x)$ of ξ_n when $\chi_n \equiv \mu$ (constant) and (a) $G(x) = 1 - e^{-\lambda x}$ if $x \geq 0$, (b) $G(x) = 1 - e^{-\lambda(x-\tau)}$ if $x \geq \tau$ and $G(x) = 0$ otherwise.

Note: Knowing $P(x)$, we can obtain formulae of correction theory for particle counting with electron-multipliers and Geiger–Müller counters.

22. We select m points which are independently and uniformly distributed over the interval $(0, 1)$. Let $\xi_1, \xi_2, \ldots, \xi_m$ denote their coordinates arranged in an increasing order. Show that the sequence of random variables $\{\xi_n\}$, $(n = 1, 2, \ldots, m)$ has a Markov character and determine the transition probabilities $\mathbf{P}\{\xi_n \leq x \mid \xi_{n-1} = y\}$.

23. *Waiting-time problem.* Customers arrive to a server at the instants $\tau_0, \tau_1, \ldots, \tau_n, \ldots$ The server attends them in the order in which they arrive. Denote by $\chi_0, \chi_1, \ldots, \chi_n, \ldots$ the durations of the successive services. Suppose that the time intervals $\tau_n - \tau_{n-1}$ $(n = 1, 2, 3, \ldots)$ and the service-times χ_n $(n = 0, 1, 2, \ldots)$ are independent sequences of independent, positive random variables with distribution functions $F(x)$ and $H(x)$ respectively.

Denote by the random variable ξ_n $(n = 0, 1, 2, \ldots)$ the waiting time of the customer who arrives at the instant τ_n. Under what conditions have the random variables $\{\xi_n\}$ a limiting distribution and how can this be found?

9. Stationary stochastic sequences. A sequence of real random variables $\{\xi_n\}$ $(n = 0, \pm 1, \pm 2, \ldots)$ is called a *stationary stochastic sequence* (in the wider sense) if the expectation and variance of ξ_n exist and are independent of n and the correlation coefficient of ξ_n and ξ_m depends only on the difference $m - n$.

Thus stationary Markov chains are special cases of stationary stochastic sequences, provided that the stationary distribution has a finite variance.

Let $\mathbf{E}\{\xi_n\} = a$, $\mathbf{D}^2\{\xi_n\} = \sigma^2$ and

$$\mathbf{R}\{\xi_n, \xi_m\} = [\mathbf{E}\{\xi_n \xi_m\} - a^2]/\sigma^2 = R(m - n).$$

For the correlation function $R(n)$ of a stationary sequence it holds that $R(-n) = R(n)$ and $R(n)$ can always be expressed in the form

$$(33) \qquad R(n) = \int_{-\pi}^{\pi} e^{i\lambda n} \, dF(\lambda),$$

where $F(\lambda)$, $(-\pi \leq \lambda \leq \pi)$ is a distribution function. $F(\lambda)$ is called the *spectral distribution function* of the sequence $\{\xi_n\}$. On the other hand, all such functions $R(n)$ can be regarded as correlation functions of a stationary stochastic sequence.

If

$$\sum_{n=0}^{\infty} |R(n)| < \infty,$$

then $F'(\lambda) = f(\lambda)$ exists and $f(\lambda)$ is called the *spectral density function* of the sequence. The Fourier series of $f(\lambda)$ is

$$(34) \qquad f(\lambda) = \frac{1}{2\pi} \sum_{n=-\infty}^{\infty} R(n)e^{-in\lambda}, \qquad (-\pi \leq \lambda \leq \pi).$$

One of the most frequent problems arising in connection with stationary stochastic sequences is the *linear prediction* of the sequence, that is, for a given m $(m \geq 0)$ it is to be determined the best linear approximation of $\xi_{n \mid m}$ by means of $\xi_{n-1}, \xi_{n-2}, \ldots$ On the principle of least squares we can formulate the problem of linear extrapolation as follows: to determine the real constants $a_1, a_2, \ldots$ for a given m in such a way that the random variable

$$L_m(n) = \sum_{k=1}^{\infty} a_k \xi_{n-k}$$

shall approximate to ξ_{n+m} better than any other random variable, when their mean-square errors are compared; that is, to determine the constants so that $\mathbf{E}\{[\xi_{n+m} - L_m(n)]^2\}$ is minimal. Let this minimum be σ_m^2.

When $F(\lambda)$ is the spectral distribution function of the stationary stochastic sequence $\{\xi_n\}$, the following conditions can be used to determine the constants $a_1, a_2, \ldots$:

$$\int_{-\pi}^{\pi} e^{ik\lambda}[e^{im\lambda} - \Phi_m(\lambda)] \, dF(\lambda) = 0, \quad (k = 0, 1, 2, \ldots)$$

where

$$\Phi_m(\lambda) = \sum_{k=1}^{\infty} a_k e^{-ik\lambda}.$$

Furthermore, in this case

$$\sigma_m^2/\sigma^2 = 1 - \int_{-\pi}^{\pi} | \Phi_m(\lambda) |^2 \, dF(\lambda).$$

When the sequence $\{\xi_n\}$ has a spectral density function $f(\lambda)$ and this is a rational function of $z = e^{i\lambda}$, then the unknowns $a_1, a_2, \ldots$ can be determined by the methods of the theory of complex functions. Let $f(\lambda) = f^*(e^{i\lambda})$, where $f^*(z)$ is a rational function of z and

$$\Phi_m^*(z) = \sum_{k=1}^{\infty} a_k z^{-k}.$$ Then $\Phi_m^*(z)$ is uniquely determined by the following requirements:

1. $\Phi_m^*(z)$ is regular on and outside the unit circle.
2. $\Phi_m^*(\infty) = 0$.
3. $[z^m - \Phi_m^*(z)]f^*(z)$ is regular on and inside the unit circle.

Problems for solution

24. If $R(n) = a^{|n|}$, where a is real and $| a | < 1$, can $R(n)$ be the correlation function of a stationary sequence?

25. Show that $R(n)$ of Problem 24 is the correlation function of the sequence

$$\xi_n = \sqrt{1 - a^2} \sum_{k=0}^{\infty} a^k \eta_{n-k}$$

if $\{\eta_n\}$ is a sequence of uncorrelated random variables with mean-value 0 and variance 1.

26. Let

$$f(\lambda) = \frac{C}{2\pi} \frac{| e^{i\lambda} - b |^2}{| e^{i\lambda} - a |^2} = \frac{C}{2\pi} \frac{(e^{i\lambda} - b)(e^{-i\lambda} - b)}{(e^{i\lambda} - a)(e^{-i\lambda} - a)}$$

with a suitably chosen constant C, where a and b are real numbers and $| a | < 1$, $| b | < 1$. Determine $R(n)$.

27. Linear extrapolation. Suppose that the stationary stochastic sequence $\{\xi_n\}$ possesses a spectral density function

$$f(\lambda) = \frac{C}{2\pi} \frac{| e^{i\lambda} - b |^2}{| e^{i\lambda} - a |^2}$$

where a and b are real constants for which $|a| < 1$, and $|b| < 1$. Determine the real constants $a_1, a_2, a_2, \ldots$ for a given m in such a way that

$$L_m(n) = \sum_{k=1}^{\infty} a_k \xi_{n-k}$$

shall minimize the mean-square error of the prediction for ξ_{n+m}.

CHAPTER 2

MARKOV PROCESSES

---

1. Introduction. If we are interested in the development in time of a physical system and if we characterise the state of the system with variables $\xi_0, \xi_1, \ldots, \xi_n, \ldots$ at times $t = 0, 1, \ldots, n, \ldots$, then these variables $\{\xi_n\}$ will form a stochastic sequence. However, in many cases we would like to know the exact development in time of the system. For this purpose we introduce the random variables ξ_t, which characterises the state of the system at every instant t over a finite or infinite interval of the real parameter t. The family of random variables $\{\xi_t\}$ forms a stochastic process. As in the case of stochastic sequences where Markov chains played an important role, so amongst the stochastic processes the processes of Markovian type have a broad field of application.

2. Definition of Markov processes. Consider a family of real random variables $\{\xi_t\}$ where the range of the parameter t is a finite or an infinite interval.

The stochastic process $\{\xi_t\}$ is called a Markov process if

$$(1) \quad \mathbf{P}\{\xi_t \leq x \mid \xi_{t_1} = y_1, \xi_{t_2} = y_2, \ldots, \xi_{t_n} = y_n\} = \mathbf{P}\{\xi_t \leq x \mid \xi_{t_n} = y_n\}$$

holds for all $t_1 < t_2 < \ldots < t_n < t$ $(n = 1, 2, \ldots)$ and for all possible values of the random variables in question.

The stochastic behaviour of a Markov process is uniquely determined by the *initial distribution* $\mathbf{P}\{\xi_0 \leq x\} = P(0, x)$ and the following conditional distribution functions:

$$(2) \quad \mathbf{P}\{\xi_t \leq x \mid \xi_s = y\} = F(s, y; t, x), \quad \text{(where } s < t\text{),}$$

which are called *transition probabilities*.

In particular the distribution function $\mathbf{P}\{\xi_t \leq x\} = P(t, x)$ is given by

$$P(t, x) = \int_{-\infty}^{\infty} F(0, y; t, x) \, d_y P(0, y).$$

By the theorem of total probability we can easily show the validity of the so-called *Chapman–Kolmogorov* equation:

$$(3) \quad F(s, y; t, x) = \int_{-\infty}^{\infty} F(u, z; t, x) \, d_z F(s, y; u, z), \quad (s < u < t).$$

A Markov process $\{\xi_t\}$ is called *homogeneous* in time when the transition probabilities $F(s, y; t, x)$ depend only on $t - s$ apart from y and x. The Markov process $\{\xi_t\}$ is called *additive* (or process with independent increments or differential process) when the transition probabilities $F(s, y; t, x)$ depend only on $x - y$ apart from s and t; in this case $\xi_t - \xi_s$ will be independent of all those ξ_u for which $u \leq s$.

A Markov process $\{\xi_t\}$ is called *ergodic* when the limiting distribution function $\lim\limits_{t \to \infty} \mathbf{P}\{\xi_t \leq x \mid \xi_0 = y\}$ exists irrespective of y. In this case $\lim\limits_{t \to \infty} \mathbf{P}\{\xi_t \leq x\}$ also exists, independent of the initial distribution and agrees with the former one.

$P^*(x)$ is called a *stationary distribution* if when it is chosen for an initial distribution $P(0, x) = P^*(x)$ the distributions $P(t, x)$ for all t are equal to $P^*(x)$.

Another classification of the Markov processes $\{\xi_t\}$ can be made according to whether ξ_t varies by jumps or continuously or both by jumps and continuously.

3. Poisson process.

The simplest special case of a Markov process is the Poisson process. Suppose that the Markov process $\{\xi_t\}$ is homogeneous and additive, the differences $\xi_t - \xi_s$ are non-negative integers for all values of $s < t$, and furthermore, that

$$(4) \quad \lim_{\Delta t \to 0} \frac{\mathbf{P}\{\xi_{t+\Delta t} - \xi_t > 1\}}{\mathbf{P}\{\xi_{+\Delta t} - \xi_t = 1\}} = 0.$$

In this case $\{\xi_t\}$ is said to form a homogeneous Poisson process.

If $\xi_0 \equiv 0$, then we can regard the variable ξ_t as the number of random events which occur in the interval $(0, t)$. With this interpretation condition (4) means that the probability that in a very short time more than one event occur is very small compared with the probability that exactly one event occurs. If $\xi_0 \equiv 0$, then let $\mathbf{P}\{\xi_t = n\} = P_n(t)$ for $t \geq 0$. Then in the general case

$$\mathbf{P}\{\xi_t - \xi_s = n\} = P_n(t - s).$$

Theorem 1. If $\{\xi_t\}$ is a homogeneous Poisson process, then there exists a constant $\lambda \geq 0$ such that

$$(5) \qquad P_n(t) = e^{-\lambda t} \frac{(\lambda t)^n}{n!}, \qquad (n = 0, 1, 2, \ldots).$$

Proof: Owing to the additivity of the process $\{\xi_t\}$ the random variables $\xi_{u+t} - \xi_u$ and $\xi_{u+t+s} - \xi_{u+t}$ are independent if $t > 0$ and $s > 0$, and therefore

$$\mathbf{P}\{\xi_{u+t+s} - \xi_u = 0\} = \mathbf{P}\{\xi_{u+t} - \xi_u = 0\}\mathbf{P}\{\xi_{u+t+s} - \xi_{u+t} = 0\},$$

that is,

$$P_0(t + s) = P_0(t)P_0(s).$$

Since $P_0(s) \leq 1$, consequently $P_0(t + s) \leq P_0(t)$, i.e. $P_0(t)$ is a monotone non-increasing function. Hence $P_0(t) = e^{-\lambda t}$ (where $\lambda \geq 0$) will be the only solution of this functional equation. This proves (5) for $n = 0$. If $\lambda = 0$, then $P_0(t) = 1$ and consequently $P_n(t) = 0$ if $n = 1, 2, \ldots$ Let us consider the case $\lambda > 0$. According to the total probability theorem we can write

$$P_n(t + s) = \sum_{j=0}^{n} P_j(t)P_{n-j}(s).$$

Now $\lim_{s \to 0} \dfrac{1 - P_0(s)}{s} = \lambda$ and so according to (4) we shall have

$$\lim_{s \to 0} \frac{P_1(s)}{s} = \lambda, \quad \lim_{s \to 0} \frac{P_n(s)}{s} = 0 \text{ (for } n > 1).$$

Forming the limit $\lim_{s \to 0} \dfrac{P_n(t + s) - P_n(t)}{s}$, by means of the above equations we obtain a system of differential equations

$$\frac{dP_n(t)}{dt} = -\lambda P_n(t) + \lambda P_{n-1}(t), \qquad (n = 1, 2, \ldots)$$

to determine the unknowns $P_n(t)$. Now $P_0(t) = e^{-\lambda t}$ and $P_n(0) = 0$ ($n = 1, 2, \ldots$). Knowing these initial conditions the system of differential equations determines $P_1(t)$, $P_2(t)$, $\ldots$, $P_n(t)$, $\ldots$ in succession, and the solutions are found to be in accordance with equation (5).

In this case the transition probability $F(s, y; t, x)$ is a step function of x, namely,

$$F(s, y; t, x) = \sum_{n=0}^{[x-y]} \frac{\lambda^n(t - s)^n}{n!} e^{-\lambda(t-s)},$$

if y is a non-negative integer, $y \le x$ and $s < t$.

Remark: Omitting the assumption of homogeneity, we find that there exists a monotone non-decreasing continuous function $\Lambda(t)$ for which

$$(6) \qquad \mathbf{P}\{\xi_t - \xi_s = n\} = e^{-[\Lambda(t)-\Lambda(s)]} \frac{[\Lambda(t) - \Lambda(s)]^n}{n!}.$$

In particular, if $\Lambda(t) - \Lambda(s) = \lambda(t - s)$, then we obtain the homogeneous Poisson process.

4. Markov process with a finite or denumerably infinite number of states. Suppose that a physical system possesses a finite or denumerably infinite number of states E_1, E_2, $\ldots$, E_j, $\ldots$, and let $\xi_t = j$ if the system is in the state E_j at the instant t. Now we define the *transition probabilities* as follows:

$$(7) \qquad \mathbf{P}\{\xi_t = j \mid \xi_s = i\} = P_{ij}(s, t), \qquad (s < t).$$

The transition probabilities defined by (2) can be expressed as follows:

$$F(s, y; t, x) = \sum_{j \le x} P_{yj}(s, t).$$

The *Chapman–Kolmogorov* equation in this case will take the following simpler form which is equivalent to equation (3):

$$(8) \qquad P_{ik}(s, t) = \sum_j P_{ij}(s, u)P_{jk}(u, t).$$

The Kolmogorov equations. Suppose that

1°. To each state E_j there corresponds a continuous function

$c_j(t) \geq 0$ such that

$$(9) \qquad \lim_{\Delta t \to 0} \frac{1 - P_{jj}(t, t + \Delta t)}{\Delta t} = c_j(t)$$

holds uniformly in t.

This condition means: If at the instant t the system is in the state E_j, then the probability that during $(t, t + \Delta t)$ a transition occurs is $c_j(t)\Delta t + o(\Delta t)$.

2°. To any two different states E_j and E_k there correspond transition probabilities $p_{jk}(t)$ such that

$$(10) \qquad \lim_{\Delta t \to 0} \frac{P_{j,k}(t, t + \Delta t)}{\Delta t} = c_j(t)p_{jk}(t)$$

holds uniformly in t, $p_{jk}(t)$ are continuous functions in t, $p_{jj}(t) = 0$; and for every fixed t and j we have

$$(11) \qquad \sum_k p_{jk}(t) = 1.$$

$p_{jk}(t)$ is the conditional probability of the event that if a transition from E_j occurs during $(t, t + \Delta t)$ then this will take the system from E_j to E_k.

$3°$. The passage to the limit in equation (10) is uniform in j for fixed k.

Under the conditions 1°, 2°, 3° we have *Kolmogorov's first system of differential equations*:

$$(12) \qquad \frac{\partial P_{ik}(s, t)}{\partial t} = -c_k(t)P_{ik}(s, t) + \sum_{j \neq k} P_{ij}(s, t)c_j(t)p_{jk}(t).$$

This can be proved by forming the limit

$$\lim_{\Delta t \to 0} \frac{P_{ik}(s, t + \Delta t) - P_{ik}(s, t)}{\Delta t}$$

while taking into consideration that

$$P_{ik}(s, t + \Delta t) = \sum_j P_{ij}(s, t)P_{jk}(t, t + \Delta t).$$

The i and s are parameters which are included in the system of differential equations (12) only through the initial conditions

$$P_{ik}(s, s) = \begin{cases} 1 & \text{if} \quad k = i \\ 0 & \text{if} \quad k \neq i. \end{cases}$$

Similarly under conditions 1° and 2° we have *Kolmogorov's second system of differential equations*

(13) $$\frac{\partial P_{ik}(s, t)}{\partial s} = c_i(s)P_{ik}(s, t) - c_i(s) \sum_{j \neq i} p_{ij}(s)P_{jk}(s, t).$$

This system can be obtained by forming the limit

$$\lim_{\Delta s \to 0} \frac{P_{ik}(s - \Delta s, t) - P_{ik}(s, t)}{\Delta s}$$

and taking into consideration that

$$P_{ik}(s - \Delta s, t) = \sum_j P_{ij}(s - \Delta s, s)P_{jk}(s, t).$$

The initial conditions are

$$P_{i,k}(t, t) = \begin{cases} 1 & \text{if} \quad i = k \\ 0 & \text{if} \quad i \neq k. \end{cases}$$

Both (12) and (13) uniquely determine the transition probabilities $P_{ik}(s, t)$ and these probabilities satisfy the relation (8) and the initial conditions.

We remark that it may happen that $\{P_{ik}(s, t)\}$ is not a true probability distribution in k, that is,

$$\sum_k P_{ik}(s, t) < 1.$$

In this case $1 - \sum_k P_{ik}(s, t)$ is the probability that an infinity of transitions has taken place during (s, t).

If $\mathbf{P}\{\xi_t = k\} = P_k(t)$ denotes the probability distribution of the random variable ξ_t, then knowing the initial distribution $\{P_i(0)\}$, we can write

$$P_k(t) = \sum_i P_i(0)P_{ik}(0, t).$$

According to equation (12), $P_k(t)$ will satisfy the following system of differential equations:

$$(14) \quad \frac{dP_k(t)}{dt} = - c_k(t)P_k(t) + \sum_{j \neq k} c_j(t)p_{jk}(t)P_j(t), \quad (k = 0, 1, 2, \ldots).$$

If the Markov process $\{\xi_t\}$ is homogeneous, then $c_j(t) \equiv c_j$ and $p_{jk}(t) \equiv p_{jk}$ are constants independent of t. For this case we can write $P_{ik}(s, t) = P_{ik}(t - s)$, and so the *first system of differential equations* will take the following form:

$$(15) \quad \frac{dP_{ik}(t)}{dt} = - c_k P_{ik}(t) + \sum_{j \neq k} c_j p_{jk} P_{ij}(t),$$

and the *second system of differential equations* will be

$$(16) \quad \frac{dP_{ik}(t)}{dt} = - c_i P_{ik}(t) + c_i \sum_{j \neq i} p_{ij} P_{jk}(t).$$

Equations (15) and (16) can be expressed also in matrix notation. Let $\mathbf{P}(t) = \| P_{ik}(t) \|$ and $\mathbf{A} = \| a_{ij} \|$, where $a_{ij} = c_i p_{ij}(i \neq j)$ and $a_{ii} = - c_i$. According to equation (15) we have

$$(17) \quad \frac{d\mathbf{P}(t)}{dt} = \mathbf{P}(t)\mathbf{A},$$

and according to (16)

$$(18) \quad \frac{d\mathbf{P}(t)}{dt} = \mathbf{A}\mathbf{P}(t).$$

The initial condition is $\mathbf{P}(0) = \mathbf{I}$, where $\mathbf{I}$ is the unit matrix.

If the number of the states is finite then the solution of matrix equations (17) and (18) can be given in the following form

$$(19) \qquad\qquad \mathbf{P}(t) = e^{\mathbf{A}t}.$$

According to (14) the absolute probabilities $\mathbf{P}\{\xi_t = k\} = P_k(t)$ satisfy the following system of differential equations:

$$(20) \quad \frac{dP_k(t)}{dt} = - c_k P_k(t) + \sum_{j \neq k} c_j p_{jk} P_j(t).$$

A homogeneous Markov process $\{\xi_t\}$ is ergodic if the limits

$$\lim_{\to \infty} P_{jk}(t) = P_k$$

exist irrespective of j and if $\{P_k\}$ is a probability distribution. If

$\{\xi\}$ is ergodic, then

$$\lim_{t \to \infty} P_k(t) = P_k$$

also holds and is independent of the initial distribution. The limiting distribution $\{P_k\}$ is uniquely determined by solving the system of linear equations

$$(21) \qquad c_k P_k = \sum_{j \neq k} c_j p_{jk} P_j.$$

If the number of states of a Markov process $\{\xi_t\}$ is finite and every state can be reached from every other state with positive probability, then $\{\xi_t\}$ is ergodic and the limiting distribution $\{P_k\}$ can be uniquely determined by solving (21).

5. Markov process with continuous transition. Let us suppose that the states of a system are characterised by the real parameter x, and let $\xi_t = x$ if x describes the state of the system at time t. Let us suppose, moreover, that the transition probabilities $F(s, y; t, x)$ are absolutely continuous functions in x. In this case we can write

$$(22) \qquad F(s, y; t, x) = \int_{-\infty}^{x} f(s, y; t, x)\, dx,$$

where $f(s, y; t, x) \geq 0$ and

$$\int_{-\infty}^{\infty} f(s, y; t, x)\, dx = 1.$$

Corresponding to the *Chapman–Kolmogorov* equation the following equation will now hold:

$$(23) \qquad f(s, y; t, x) = \int_{-\infty}^{\infty} f(s, y; u, z) f(u, z; t, x)\, dz.$$

The function $f(s, y; t, x)$ is the *transition probability density function*.

We remark that a stochastic process is called *continuous* if

$$\lim_{\Delta t \to 0} \frac{\mathbf{P}\{\,|\xi_{t+\Delta t} - \xi_t| > \varepsilon\,\}}{\Delta t} = 0$$

holds for every $\varepsilon > 0$.

Kolmogorov equations. Let us assume that the following limits exist for arbitrary $\varepsilon > 0$:

$$(24) \quad \lim_{\Delta t \to 0} \frac{1}{\Delta t} \int_{|x-y|>\varepsilon} f(t, y; t + \Delta t, x) \, dy = 0,$$

$$(25) \quad \lim_{\Delta t \to 0} \frac{1}{\Delta t} \int_{|x-y|<\varepsilon} (x - y)f(t, y; t + \Delta t, x) \, dy = a(t, x),$$

$$(26) \quad \lim_{\Delta t \to 0} \frac{1}{\Delta t} \int_{|x-y|<\varepsilon} (x - y)^2 f(t, y; t + \Delta t, x) \, dy = b(t, x) > 0.$$

It follows from (24) that the process $\{\xi_t\}$ is continuous. The dependence of (25) and (26) on ε is only apparent.

Furthermore, we suppose that the derivatives

$$(27) \quad \frac{\partial f(s, y; t, x)}{\partial y}, \qquad \frac{\partial^2 f(s, y; t, x)}{\partial y^2}$$

exist and are continuous functions of y.

Now provided that (24), (25), (26) and (27) hold, and using (23) we can obtain *Kolmogorov's first differential equation*:

$$(28) \quad \frac{\partial f(s, y; t, x)}{\partial s} + a(s, y)\frac{\partial f(s, y; t, x)}{\partial y} + \frac{1}{2}b(s, y)\frac{\partial^2 f(s, y; t, x)}{\partial y^2} = 0.$$

Similarly we can obtain *Kolmogorov's second differential equation*:

$$(29) \quad \frac{\partial f(s, y; t, x)}{\partial t} + \frac{\partial a(t, x)f(s, y; t, x)}{\partial x} - \frac{1}{2}\frac{\partial^2 b(t, x)f(s, y; t, x)}{\partial x^2} = 0.$$

The differential equations (28) or (29) determine $f(s, y; t, x)$ uniquely and their solution satisfies (23).

If the process $\{\xi_t\}$ is homogeneous and additive, then we can write $f(s, y; t, x) = g(t - s, x - y)$ and in this case $a(t, x) \equiv a$, $b(t, x) \equiv b$ are constants. In this case (28) and (29) reduce to the same partial differential equation:

$$(30) \quad \frac{\partial g(t, x)}{\partial t} + a\frac{\partial g(t, x)}{\partial x} - \frac{b}{2}\frac{\partial^2 g(t, x)}{\partial x^2} = 0.$$

6. Mixed Markov processes. Suppose that a Markov process $\{\xi_t\}$ can assume only real values and that changes can occur either continuously or by jumps. In this case the transition probabilities $F(s, y; t, x)$ can be expressed as follows:

$$(31) \quad F(t, y; t + \Delta t, x) = [1 - p(t, y)\Delta t]G(t, y; t + \Delta t, x) \\ + p(t, y)P(t, y, x)\Delta t + o(\Delta t),$$

where $p(t, y)$ and $P(t, y, x)$ are non-negative functions, $P(t, y, x)$ is a distribution function in x and $G(s, y; t, x)$ is the transition probability function of a continuous Markov process. The functions in question can be interpreted as follows: If $\xi_t = y$, then $p(t, y)\Delta t + o(\Delta t)$ is the probability that during $(t, t + \Delta t)$ a jump occurs and $P(t, y, x)$ is the probability that after a jump, if it occurs at time t, we have $\xi_{t+0} \leq x$. $G(s, y; t, x)$ is the transition probability function corresponding to the continuous change of the system.

We assume that $p(t, y)$ and $P(t, y, x)$ are continuous functions of t and that $G(s, y; t, x)$ satisfies the following conditions:

$$(32) \quad \lim_{\Delta t \to 0} \frac{1}{\Delta t} \int_{|x-y| > \varepsilon} d_y\, G(t, y; t + \Delta t, x) = 0,$$

$$(33) \quad \lim_{\Delta t \to 0} \frac{1}{\Delta t} \int_{|x-y| < \varepsilon} (x - y)d_y G(t, y; t + \Delta t, x) = a(t, x),$$

$$(34) \quad \lim_{\Delta t \to 0} \frac{1}{\Delta t} \int_{|x-y| < \varepsilon} (x - y)^2 d_y G(t, y; t + \Delta t, x) = b(t, x)$$

for arbitrary $\varepsilon > 0$. Furthermore, we suppose that

$$\frac{\partial F(s, y; t, x)}{\partial y}, \qquad \frac{\partial^2 F(s, y; t, x)}{\partial y^2}$$

exist and are continuous functions of y. In this case we have the *first integro-differential equation of Kolmogorov–Feller*:

$$(35) \quad \frac{\partial F(s, y; t, x)}{\partial s} + a(s, y)\frac{\partial F(s, y; t, x)}{\partial y} + \frac{1}{2}b(s, y)\frac{\partial^2 F(s, y; t, x)}{\partial y^2}$$

$$- p(s, y)[F(s, y; t, x) - \int_{-\infty}^{\infty} F(s, z; t, x)\, d_z P(t, y, z)] = 0,$$

and the *second integro-differential equation of Kolmogorov–Feller*:

$$(36) \quad \frac{\partial F(s, y; t, x)}{\partial t} + a(t, x)\frac{\partial F(s, y; t, x)}{\partial x} - \frac{1}{2}\frac{\partial}{\partial x}\left(b(t, x)\frac{\partial F(s, y; t, x)}{\partial x}\right)$$

$$+ \int_{-\infty}^{x} p(t, z)\, d_z F(s, y; t, z) - \int_{-\infty}^{\infty} p(t, z)P(t, z, x)\, d_z F(s, y; t, z) = 0.$$

D

The transition probability $F(s, y; t, x)$ can be determined from (35) or (36) and the solution satisfies (3).

Problems for solution

1. Let the random variable ξ_t denote the number of atoms disintegrating in a radioactive substance during the interval $(0, t)$. If we suppose that the number of atoms in the substance is very large and that the decay coefficient is small compared to the time range involved, then $\{\xi_t\}$ can be regarded as a homogeneous Poisson process. In this case $\mathbf{P}\{\xi_t = n\} = e^{-\lambda t}(\lambda t)^n/n!$, where λ is a positive constant. Discuss the different meanings of λ.

2. Let $\{\xi_t\}$ be a homogeneous Poisson process with density λ. Denote by $\{\tau_n\}$ the sequence of the instants of the occurrence of the random events. Prove that the time differences

$$\tau_{n+1} - \tau_n \ (n = 0, 1, \ldots; \tau_0 = 0)$$

are identically distributed independent random variables with distribution function $F(x) = 1 - e^{-\lambda x}$ for $x \geq 0$ and $F(x) = 0$ for $x < 0$.

3. Let $\{\xi_t\}$ be a homogeneous Poisson process with density λ. Let the random variable η_t be defined as the length of time elapsing from t to the occurrence of the next random event. Prove that $\mathbf{P}\{\eta_t \leq x\} = 1 - e^{-\lambda x}$ for $x \geq 0$.

4. Let us suppose that the events of a Poisson process $\{\xi_t\}$, with density λ, are filtered in such a way that each event of the process is cancelled with probability $1 - p$ and left unchanged with probability p, the cancelling (or not cancelling) of any event being independent of the cancelling (or not cancelling) of any other event. Let ζ_t denote the number of remaining events during the time interval $(0, t)$ and prove that $\{\zeta_t\}$ is a Poisson process with density λp. (This situation arises if the disintegrations of radioactive atoms in a radioactive substance form a Poisson process with density λ but an emitted particle passes through the counter tube only with probability p. In this case the registrations of the particles also form a Poisson process, but with density λp.)

5. **Rutherford, Chadwick and Ellis** observed in $N = 2,608$ cases the number of those particles which reached the counter tube from a

radioactive substance during time intervals of $t = 7.5$ seconds each. They found that the counter recorded k particles in N_k cases, where

k	0	1	2	3	4	5	6	7	8	9	≥ 10
N_k	57	203	383	525	532	408	273	139	45	27	16

Does the assumption of a Poisson process explain these observed values?

6. Prove that if $\{\xi_t\}$ and $\{\eta_t\}$ are two independent Poisson processes with densities λ and μ respectively, then $\{\xi_t + \eta_t\}$ is again a Poisson process with density $\lambda + \mu$. (For example, if we examine radioactive decay with a particle counter and λ is the density of particle arrivals to the counter, and the experiment is perturbed by the cosmic radiation which passes through the tube and which is assumed to follow a Poisson process with density μ, then the counter tube will register as if it were counting particles emitted according to a Poisson process with density $\lambda + \mu$.)

7. Let us denote by ξ_t the number of events which occur in a Poisson process with density λ during $(0, t)$ and by $\tau_1, \tau_2, \ldots$ $\tau_n, \ldots$ the times at which these events occur. Prove that, under the condition $\xi_t = n$, the joint distribution of the instants $\tau_1, \tau_2, \ldots, \tau_n$ is the same as the joint distribution of the coordinates arranged in increasing order of n independent points, each of which is uniformly distributed over the interval $(0, t)$.

8. The electron emission from the cathode of an electronic tube follows a Poisson process with density λ.

Let us suppose the times of flight of the electrons to be independent of each other with the same distribution function $F(x)$. We observe the phenomena in the time interval $(0, \infty)$ and denote by η_t the number of electrons present in the tube at time t. Determine the probability distribution of η_t and its limit as $t \to \infty$.

9. Let us denote by ξ_t the number of events which occur in a Poisson process with density λ during $(0, t)$. Determine the correlation coefficient of ξ_t and $\xi_{t+\tau}$.

10. Let us suppose $\{\xi_t\}$ to be a homogeneous, additive Markov process, and the differences $\xi_t - \xi_s$ to be non-negative integers for

$s < t$. In this case $\{\xi_t\}$ is called *compound Poisson process*. Determine the distribution of $\xi_t - \xi_s$.

11. Consider the Borel measurable sets $\{A\}$ of a finite dimensional Euclidean space. Let $\mu(A)$ be the Lebesgue-measure of A. With each measurable set A, with $\mu(A) < \infty$, let there be associated a random variable $\xi(A)$ which takes only non-negative integral values, and has the following properties: 1°. The distribution of $\xi(A)$ depends only on the measure $\mu(A)$ and $\mathbf{P}\{\xi(A) = 0\} \neq 1$ if $\mu(A) > 0$. 2°. If A_1 and A_2 are disjoint sets, then

$$\xi(A_1 + A_2) = \xi(A_1) + \xi(A_2)$$

and $\xi(A_1)$ and $\xi(A_2)$ are independent. 3°. If $\mu(A) \longrightarrow 0$ then

$$\mathbf{P}\{\xi(A) \geqq 1\}/\mathbf{P}\{\xi(A) = 1\} \longrightarrow 1.$$

Prove that

$$\mathbf{P}\{\xi(A) = n\} = e^{-\lambda\mu(A)} [\lambda\mu(A)]^n/n!, \qquad (n = 0, 1, 2, \ldots),$$

where λ is a positive constant.

12. We can apply the conditions of Problem 11 to the spatial distribution of stars, where now $\xi(A)$ is the number of stars in the region A. Determine the distribution function and the mean value for the distance of a star from the nearest one.

13. The instants of the events of a Poisson process with density λ which occur during $(0, t)$ are represented on a circle whose circumference is of length t. ξ_t denotes the number of events. Intervals of length α are marked on the circumference of the circle starting from points associated with the events. Let η_t denote the numbers of points which are not covered by any of these intervals. Determine the distribution of η_t.

14. Denote by $\tau_1, \tau_2, \ldots, \tau_n, \ldots$ the instants of the events occurring in a Poisson process with density λ in the time interval $0 \leq t < \infty$. Determine the distribution function $G_n(t)$, the density function $g_n(t)$, and the moments of the random variable τ_n $(n = 1, 2, \ldots)$.

15. Let $E_0, E_1, \ldots, E_n, \ldots$ be the possible states of a Markov process. Let $\xi_t = n$ if the system is in the state E_n at time t. Let us suppose that the probability that during $(t, t + \Delta t)$ a transition occurs is $c_n(t)\Delta t + o(\Delta t) = \lambda\Delta t + o(\Delta t)$ given that the system is in the state E_n at time t. Further suppose that $E_n \longrightarrow E_{n+1}(n = 0,$

1, 2, . . .) are the only possible transitions and that $p_{n, n+1}(t) = 1$. Prove that $\{\xi_t\}$ is a homogeneous Poisson process.

16. *Erlang's formula.* Let us suppose that at a telephone exchange calls are arriving according to a Poisson process with density λ. The telephone exchange has m available channels. Suppose that a connection is realised if the incoming call finds an idle channel. If all channels are busy, then the incoming call is lost. Let us suppose that the holding times are independent, positive random variables with the same distribution function $H(x) = 1 - e^{-\mu x}$ (for $x \geq 0$). Denote by ξ_t the number of busy channels at the moment t. We say that the system is in the state E_n $(n = 0, 1, \ldots, m)$ if n channels are busy. Determine the limiting probabilities

$$\lim_{t \to \infty} \mathbf{P}\{\xi_t = n\} = P_n \qquad (n = 0, 1, \ldots, m).$$

17. *Machine interference problem.* Let us suppose that m automatic machines are serviced by an operator. Owing to random mistakes the machines occasionally may break down and call for service. Suppose that if at time t a machine is in a working state, then the probability that it will call for service in the time interval $(t, t + \Delta t)$ is $\lambda \Delta t + o(\Delta t)$ for each machine. We assume that the machines work independently and that the operator is busy if there is a machine on the waiting line. Furthermore, we suppose that the service times are identically-distributed, independent, positive random variables with distribution function $H(x) = 1 - e^{-\mu x}$ (for $x \geq 0$). Denote by ξ_t the number of machines working at the moment t. We say that the system is in the state E_j $(j = 0, 1, \ldots, m)$ if the number of simultaneously working machines is j. Show that $\{\xi_t\}$ is a Markov process and determine the limiting probabilities

$$\lim_{t \to \infty} \mathbf{P}\{\xi_t = j\} = P_j \qquad (j = 0, 1, \ldots, m).$$

18. Consider the previous problem with the modification that now the number of operators is s, the other conditions being left unchanged. Determine the limiting probability distribution $\{P_j\}$ of the number of the working machines.

19. Let a radioactive substance contain N radioactive atoms of the same type at time $t = 0$. We assume that each atom can disintegrate with the same probability $q(t)$ during time t, provided it had not decayed earlier, and that the decay probability is independent of the starting point of this time interval. Denote by ξ_t the number of the atoms present at time t. Prove that $\{\xi_t\}$ is a Markov process and determine the distribution of ξ_t. Denote by τ_j the time instant when the number of atoms decreases to j. Determine the expectation of the random variable τ_j.

20. A counter tube starts giving out impulses at $t = 0$ according to a Poisson process with density λ. There is a scaler before the register which allows through only every m-th impulse. Denote by ξ_t the number of impulses during $(0, t)$ and by η_t the number of registrations during $(0, t)$. Determine the limit

$$\lim_{t \to \infty} \mathbf{P}\{\eta_{t+u} - \eta_t = n\}.$$

21. Let us suppose that an electric circuit supplies m machines which use the current only intermittently. Let us assume that the machines work independently of each other and that if a machine is not working at time t, then with probability $\lambda \Delta t + o(\Delta t)$ it will call for current during $(t, t + \Delta t)$. Let us suppose that the working periods are independent positive random variables with the same distribution function $H(x) = 1 - e^{-\mu x}$ (for $x \geq 0$). Let $\xi_t = j$ if at time t the number of working machines is j. In this case we shall say that the system is in state E_j. Show that $\{\xi_t\}$ is a Markov process and determine $\mathbf{P}\{\xi_t = k \mid \xi_0 = i\} = P_{ik}(t)$ and $\lim_{t \to \infty} \mathbf{P}\{\xi_t = k\} = P_k$.

22. Let us suppose that calls are arriving at a telephone exchange according to a Poisson process with density λ. Suppose that the exchange has an infinite number of available channels and the holding times are independent positive random variables with the same distribution function $H(x) = 1 - e^{-\mu x}$ (for $x \geq 0$). Denote by ξ_t the number of busy channels at time t. Show that $\{\xi_t\}$ is a Markov process and determine $\mathbf{P}\{\xi_t = k \mid \xi_0 = i\} = P_{ik}(t)$ and

$$\lim_{t \to \infty} \mathbf{P}\{\xi_t = k\} = P_k.$$

23. *Cascade process.* Let us suppose that a nucleon of large energy enters our atmosphere at time $t = 0$. This nucleon gives rise to fresh nucleons by colliding with atoms in the atmosphere and likewise these secondary nuclei will also continue multiplying independently of each other. Suppose the probability that a nucleon gives rise to a secondary nucleon during time Δt is equal to $\lambda \Delta t + o(\Delta t)$. Denote by ξ_t the number of nucleons present in the atmosphere at time t. Determine the distribution of ξ_t.

24. Let $E_0, E_1, \ldots, E_n, \ldots$ be the possible states of a Markov process. Suppose that if the system is in the state E_n at time t, then the probability of a transition $E_n \longrightarrow E_{n+1}$ $(n = 0, 1, 2, \ldots)$ during $(t, t + \Delta t)$ is $\lambda_n \Delta t + o(\Delta t)$ and that no other transition can occur. At time $t = 0$ the system is in state E_0. Determine $P_n(t)$ and show

that $\displaystyle\sum_{n=0}^{\infty} P_n(t) < 1$ holds if and only if $\displaystyle\sum_{n=0}^{\infty} 1/\lambda_n$ converges.

25. *Birth and death process.* We say that a population is in state E_n at time t if the number of individuals at t is $\xi_t = n$. Let us suppose that if an individual is alive at time t, then in the time interval $(t, t + \Delta t)$ it can produce a descendant with probability $\lambda \Delta t + o(\Delta t)$ or it can die with probability $\mu \Delta t + o(\Delta t)$ independently of the other individuals. Let $\xi_0 = 1$. Determine the distribution $\{P_n(t)\}$ and the extinction probability $\lim_{t \to \infty} P_0(t) = P_0$.

26. Denote by ξ_t the number of nuclei at time t in a cosmic-ray shower which was started by a single nucleon at time $t = 0$. We speak about the system being in state E_n at time t when $\xi_t = n$. Suppose that if the system is in state E_n at time t, then the probability of a transition $E_n \longrightarrow E_{n+1}$ during $(t, t + \Delta t)$ is $n\lambda \Delta t + o(\Delta t)$ and the probability of a transition $E_n \longrightarrow E_{n-1}$ during $(t, t + \Delta t)$ is $n\mu t \Delta t + o(\Delta t)$. Determine the distribution $\{P_n(t)\}$.

27. *Pólya process.* Let the possible values of the random variables $\xi_t (0 \le t < \infty)$ be $\xi_t = n (n = 0, 1, 2, \ldots)$, in which case we say that there is a state E_n at time t. Let $\xi_0 = 0$. If the system is in state E_n at time t, then the probability of a transition $E_n \longrightarrow E_{n+1}$ during $(t, t + \Delta t)$ is $\lambda_n(t)\Delta t + o(\Delta t)$, where $\lambda_n(t) = (1 + nd)/(1 + td)$, and no other transition can occur. Determine the probability distribution $\mathbf{P}\{\xi_t = n\} = P_n(t)$, $(n = 0, 1, 2, \ldots)$.

28. *Diffusion process.* Denote by ξ_t the position of a particle at time t in the case of one-dimensional diffusion. Let the family of random variables $\{\xi_t\}$ be a continuous Markov process which is homogeneous and additive and let the transition probability density be $f(s, y; t, x)$ where $f(s, y; t, x)$ satisfies conditions (24), (25) and (26) with $a(t, x) = 0$ and $b(t, x) = 1$. Determine $f(s, y; t, x)$.

29. Suppose the process $\{\xi_t\}$ of the previous problem to be inhomogeneous but additive. In this case we have $a(t, x) = a(t)$ and $b(t, x) = b(t)$. Determine $f(s, y; t, x)$.

30. *Drifting of stones on river beds.* At time $t = 0$ a stone is placed on the bed of a river at point $x = 0$. Let $\xi_t = x$ if at time t the stone is in position x. Suppose that $\lambda \Delta t + o(\Delta t)$ is the probability of a displacement during $(t, t + \Delta t)$ independently of t and of the position of the stone. Let us suppose that the consecutive displacements are independent random variables with the same distribution function $U(x)$. Determine the distribution function $\mathbf{P}\{\xi_t \leq x\}$.

31. We count particles arriving according to a Poisson process with density λ with an electron multiplier. The multiplier produces voltage impulses at the arriving times of particles. The amplitudes of these impulses are identically distributed, independent, positive random variables with distribution function $H(x)$. The voltage on the input resistance of the amplifier decreases exponentially in time with time constant RC ($\alpha = 1/RC$). Denote by ξ_t the voltage on the input resistance at time t. Let $\xi_0 \equiv 0$. Determine $\mathbf{P}\{\xi_t \leq x\}$ and $\lim_{t \to \infty} \mathbf{P}\{\xi_t \leq x\}$.

32. *Waiting-time problem.* Customers are arriving at a server according to a Poisson process with density λ. The server attends to them in order of arrival. The consecutive service times are identically distributed, independent, positive random variables with a common distribution function $H(x)$. Denote by ξ_t the virtual waiting time, i.e. the time which a customer would wait if he joined the queue at the instant t. Let $\xi_0 \equiv 0$, and determine the limiting distribution $\lim_{t \to \infty} \mathbf{P}\{\xi_t \leq x\}$.

33. Problem of slowing down neutrons in nuclear reactors. Consider a neutron of initial energy E_0 at time $t = 0$ moving through a moderator (of infinite size) which consists of atoms of r different types. The neutron is permanently losing its energy in collisions with the nuclei of the moderator. Denote by E_t the energy of the neutron at time t and let $\xi_t = \log E_0/E_t$ be the lethargy of the neutron at time t. Let us suppose that if $\xi_t = x$, then $\lambda_i e^{-x/2}\Delta t + o(\Delta t)$ is the probability of a collision with a nucleus of type i during $(t, t + \Delta t)$ and let the distribution function of the increase of lethargy in a collision be

$$H_i(x) = \begin{cases} 0 & \text{if } x < 0, \\[2mm] \dfrac{1 - e^{-x}}{1 - \alpha_i} & \text{if } 0 \le x \le \log \dfrac{1}{\alpha_i}, \\[2mm] 1 & \text{if } x > \log \dfrac{1}{\alpha_i}, \end{cases}$$

where $\alpha_i = \left(\dfrac{A_i - 1}{A_i + 1}\right)^2$ and A_i is the mass number of the i-th nuclei. This type of collision is the so-called isotropic collision. Determine the distribution function of ξ_t and the average energy $\mathbf{E}\{E_t\}$.

34. Let $H(t) = 1 - e^{-\lambda t}$ (if $t \ge 0$) be the distribution function of the life-time of a component of a machine. Suppose that the machine is working intermittently. If at time t the machine is not working, then let $\eta \Delta t + o(\Delta t)$ be the probability that it will start to work during $(t, t + \Delta t)$, and if it is working at time t, then let $\gamma \Delta t + o(\Delta t)$ be the probability that it will stop during $(t, t + \Delta t)$. Suppose that at time $t = 0$ the machine is not working. Determine $F(t)$, the distribution function of the apparent life-time of the component and also the mean m and the variance σ^2 of this distribution.

CHAPTER 3

NON-MARKOVIAN PROCESSES

———

In the theory of non-Markovian stochastic processes we do not have similar general theorems as in the theory of Markov processes. Of the non-Markovian processes we know most about stationary processes, recurrent (or regenerative or imbedded Markovian) processes and secondary processes generated by an underlying process. It is often possible to treat a stochastic process of non-Markovian type by reducing it to a Markov process.

1. Recurrent processes. A direct generalisation of the homogeneous Poisson process leads to the simplest non-Markovian process, the so-called *recurrent process*. As we have seen in the case of homogeneous Poisson processes if $\tau_1, \tau_2, \ldots, \tau_n, \ldots$ are the instants at which a random event occurs during time $0 \leq t < \infty$, then the time differences $\tau_n - \tau_{n-1}$ ($n = 1, 2, 3, \ldots; \tau_0 = 0$) are identically-distributed, independent, positive, random variables with the distribution function $F(x) = 1 - e^{-\lambda x}$ (if $x \geq 0$). Now if, more generally, it is assumed that the time differences $\tau_n - \tau_{n-1}$ ($n = 1, 2, 3, \ldots; \tau_0 = 0$) are identically-distributed, independent, positive random variables with a common distribution function $F(x)$, and the number of events which occur during the time interval $(0, t]$ is denoted by ξ_t, then we say that $\{\xi_t\}$ forms a *recurrent process*.

Note that in general the random variable τ_1 can be permitted to have a distribution which is different from $F(x)$, in which case we speak about a *general recurrent process*. If the mean value of $F(x)$,

$$\mu = \int_0^\infty x \, dF(x),$$

is finite and

$$F^*(x) = \frac{1}{\mu} \int_0^x [1 - F(y)] \, dy$$

46

is the distribution function of τ_1, then we call $\{\xi_t\}$ a *stationary recurrent process*.

The distribution of ξ_t. Let $\mathbf{P}\{\xi_t \leq n\} = W(t, n)$. Since $\xi_t \leq n$ holds if and only if $t < \tau_{n+1}$, we can write

(1) $\quad W(t, n) = \mathbf{P}\{t < \tau_{n+1}\} = 1 - \mathbf{P}\{\tau_{n+1} \leq t\} = 1 - F_{n+1}(t),$

where $F_n(t)$ denotes the n-th iterated convolution of the distribution function $F(t)$ with itself ($F_0(t) = 1$ if $t \geq 0$ and $F_0(t) = 0$ if $t < 0$). The quantity $\tau_{n+1} = \tau_1 + (\tau_2 - \tau_1) + \ldots + (\tau_{n+1} - \tau_n)$ is a sum of $n + 1$ independent random variables each of which has a distribution function $F(x)$.

The expectation and the moments of ξ_t. Let $m(t)$ denote the expectation of the number of events occurring in the time interval $(0, t]$, that is $m(t) = \mathbf{E}\{\xi_t\}$. We have

(2) $$m(t) = \sum_{n=0}^{\infty} [1 - W(t, n)] = \sum_{n=1}^{\infty} F_n(t).$$

This follows from

$$m(t) = \sum_{n=0}^{\infty} n\mathbf{P}\{\xi_t = n\} = \sum_{n=0}^{\infty} \mathbf{P}\{\xi_t > n\}.$$

Let $m_r(t) = \mathbf{E}\{\xi_t^r\}$ be the r-th moment of the random variable ξ_t. We have

(3) $$m_r(t) = \sum_{n=0}^{\infty} n^r[W(t, n) - W(t, n - 1)]$$

$$= \sum_{n=0}^{\infty} [(n + 1)^r - n^r] F_{n+1}(t),$$

where the right-hand side is obtained by applying the method of Abel's partial summation. The above sums are convergent if $F(0) < 1$. In our case this condition is satisfied because we supposed that $F(0) = 0$.

Now $m(t) = m_1(t)$ is the expectation and $d^2(t) = m_2(t) - [m_1(t)]^2$ is the variance of the random variable ξ_t.

The functions (1), (2) and (3) can easily be determined by means of Laplace transforms. Let

$$\phi(s) = \int_0^\infty e^{-sx}\, dF(x), \qquad (\Re(s) \geqq 0),$$

then it holds for $\Re(s) > 0$ that

(4) $$\int_0^\infty e^{-st}\, W(t, n)\, dt = \frac{1 - [\phi(s)]^{n+1}}{s},$$

(5) $$\int_0^\infty e^{-st}\, dm(t) = \frac{\phi(s)}{1 - \phi(s)},$$

and

(6) $$\int_0^\infty e^{-st}\, dm_r(t) = \sum_{j=1}^{r} \mathfrak{S}_r^j \frac{j!\,[\phi(s)]^j}{[1 - \phi(s)]^j},$$

where $\mathfrak{S}_r^j$ denotes the Stirling numbers of the second kind.† The functions in question can be uniquely determined by inverting the above Laplace transforms.

Let

(7) $$\mu = \int_0^\infty x\, dF(x)$$

and

(8) $$\sigma^2 = \int_0^\infty (x - \mu)^2\, dF(x).$$

For $m(t)$ and $d^2(t)$ we have the following asymptotic formulae:

(9) $$\lim_{t \to \infty} \frac{m(t)}{t} = \frac{1}{\mu},$$

and if $\sigma^2 < \infty$, then

(10) $$\lim_{t \to \infty} \frac{d^2(t)}{t} = \frac{\sigma^2}{\mu^3}$$

(*S. Täcklind, W. L. Smith*).

† Cf. Ch. Jordan, *Calculus of Finite Differences* (Budapest, 1939; New York, 1947), p. 168.

If $F(x)$ is not a lattice distribution, and $\mu < \infty$, then for an arbitrary $h > 0$

$$(11) \qquad \lim_{t \to \infty} \frac{m(t + h) - m(t)}{h} = \frac{1}{\mu}$$

(*D. Blackwell*). If $F(x)$ is a lattice distribution with a step $d > 0$, then

$$(12) \qquad \lim_{n \to \infty} \frac{m(nd + d) - m(nd)}{d} = \frac{1}{\mu}$$

(*A. N. Kolmogorov*).

Note that if we make further restrictions on $F(x)$ (absolute continuity, etc.), then the validity of

$$(13) \qquad \lim_{t \to \infty} m'(t) = \frac{1}{\mu}$$

can also be proved (*W. Feller, W. L. Smith*).

The distribution of η_t. Denote by the random variable η_t the distance between t and the instant of the next random event. The distribution function of this random variable is

$$(14) \qquad \mathbf{P}\{\eta_t \le x\} = \int_t^{t+x} [1 - F(t + x - u)]\, dm(u).$$

This can be seen as follows. The event $\eta_t \le x$ occurs if and only if there is at least one random event in the interval $(t, t + x]$. This event can happen in several mutually exclusive ways: in the time interval $(t, t + x]$ the last event which occurs may be the 1-st, 2-nd, ... n-th, ... one. Thus by the theorem of total probability we have

$$\mathbf{P}\{\eta_t \le x\} = \sum_{n=1}^{\infty} \mathbf{P}\{t < \tau_n \le t + x < \tau_{n+1}\}$$

$$= \sum_{n=1}^{\infty} \int_t^{t+x} [1 - F(t + x - u)]\, dF_n(u),$$

which owing to (2) agrees with (14).

If $F(x)$ is not a lattice distribution function and $\mu < \infty$, then the limiting distribution $\lim_{t \to \infty} \mathbf{P}\{\eta_t \le x\} = F^*(x)$ exists and

$$(15) \qquad F^*(x) = \frac{1}{\mu} \int_0^x [1 - F(y)] \, dy$$

if $x \geq 0$. This can be seen as follows: Let

$$g_t(u) = m(t + x) - m(t + x - u)$$

for a fixed x. In this case for a fixed x we have by (14)

$$\mathbf{P}\{\eta_t \leq x\} = \int_0^x [1 - F(u)] \, dg_t(u).$$

Since $\lim_{t \to \infty} g_t(u) = \dfrac{u}{\mu}$ and $F(u)$ is a monotone non-decreasing function, therefore by estimating the upper bound and lower bound of the approximative sum of the integral it can be seen that

$$\lim_{\to \infty} \mathbf{P}\{\eta_t \leq x\} = F^*(x).$$

If $\sigma^2 < \infty$, then

$$\lim_{t \to \infty} \mathbf{E}\{\eta_t\} = \int_0^\infty x \, dF^*(x) = \frac{\sigma^2 + \mu^2}{2\mu}$$

(*W. L. Smith*).

The distribution functions (14) and (15) can also be easily determined by Laplace transforms, namely, we have

$$(16) \qquad \int_0^\infty e^{-sx} \, d_x \mathbf{P}\{\eta_t \leq x\} = [1 - \phi(s)]e^{st} \int_t^\infty e^{-su} \, dm(u)$$

and

$$(17) \qquad \int_0^\infty e^{-sx} \, dF^*(x) = \frac{1 - \phi(s)}{\mu s}.$$

Stationary process. A stationary process is obtained by assuming that $\mathbf{P}\{\tau_1 \leq x\} = F^*(x)$. Denote by ξ_t^* the number of events which occur in the stationary process in the time interval $(0, t]$.

If $F(x)$ is not a lattice distribution function and $\mu < \infty$, then the process $\{\xi\}$ for large values of t $(t \to \infty)$ has the same stochastic behaviour as $\{\xi_t^*\}$.

Let $\mathbf{P}\{\xi_t^* \leq n\} = W^*(t, n)$. For this we have

$$(18) \qquad W^*(t, n) = 1 - F^*(t) * F_n(t).$$

For $W^*(t, n) = 1 - \mathbf{P}\{\tau_{n+1} \le t\}$, and $\tau_{n+1} = \tau_1 + (\tau_2 - \tau_1) + \ldots + (\tau_{n+1} - \tau_n)$ is a sum of $n + 1$ independent random variables amongst which n have a distribution function $F(x)$ and one has a distribution function $F^*(x)$. The Laplace transform of $W^*(t, n)$ is

$$(19) \quad \int_0^\infty e^{-st} W^*(t, n) \, dt = \frac{1}{s} - \frac{[1 - \phi(s)] \, [\phi(s)]^n}{\mu s^2}, \quad (\Re(s) > 0).$$

Let $m_r^*(t) = \mathbf{E}\{\xi_t^{*r}\}$ be the r-th moment of the random variable ξ^*. For this we have

$$(20) \quad m_r^*(t) = \sum_{n=0}^\infty [(n + 1)^r - n^r] \, [1 - W^*(t, n)]$$

and its Laplace–Stieltjes transform is

$$(21) \quad \int_0^\infty e^{-st} \, dm_r^*(t) = \frac{1}{\mu s} \sum_{j=1}^r \mathfrak{S}_r^j \frac{j! [\phi(s)]^{j-1}}{[1 - \phi(s)]^{j-1}}.$$

In particular we have for the expectation $m^*(t) = m_1^*(t)$ that

$$(22) \quad m^*(t) = \sum_{n=0}^\infty [1 - W^*(t, n)] = \frac{t}{\mu}.$$

Remark: In the case of the stationary process $\{\xi_t^*\}$ the *density* of occurrence of the events is defined by $f = 1/\mu$. In the case of the process $\{\xi_t\}$ several alternative interpretations can be given for the density of occurrence of the events:

$$f = \lim_{t \to \infty} \frac{m(t)}{t} = \frac{1}{\mu}$$

always exists,

$$f = \lim_{t \to \infty} \frac{m(t + h) - m(t)}{\mu} = \frac{1}{\mu}$$

exists if $F(x)$ is not a lattice distribution function and $\mu < \infty$,

$$f = \lim_{t \to \infty} m'(t) = \frac{1}{\mu}$$

exists if $F(x)$ is absolutely continuous and certain other conditions are also satisfied.

Up to now we have dealt with the determination of the distributions and moments of the random variables ξ_t and ξ_t^* when $F(x)$ is known. However, in many applications $F(x)$ is not known or is too complicated to determine, but the average function $m(t)$ which denotes the expectation of the number of events occurring in the time interval $(0, t]$ can easily be obtained. In this case $F(x)$ can easily be calculated from $m(t)$, and after that the above method may be used to determine the moments and distributions in question. Let

$$(23) \qquad \mu(s) = \int_0^\infty e^{-st} \, dm(t), \qquad (\Re(s) > 0),$$

be the Laplace–Stieltjes transform of $m(t)$. Now according to (5) we can write

$$(24) \qquad \mu(s) = \frac{\phi(s)}{1 - \phi(s)},$$

hence

$$(25) \qquad \phi(s) = \frac{\mu(s)}{1 + \mu(s)}$$

and $F(x)$ can be uniquely determined by inversion.

In particular, the Laplace transform (4) of $W(t, n)$ is

$$\int_0^\infty e^{-st} \, W(t, n) \, dt = \frac{1}{s} - \frac{1}{s} \left[\frac{\mu(s)}{1 + \mu(s)} \right]^{n+1}$$

and the Laplace transform (19) of $W^*(t, n)$ is

$$\int_0^\infty e^{-st} \, W^*(t, n) \, dt = \frac{1}{s} - \frac{1}{\mu s^2} \frac{[\mu(s)]^n}{[1 + \mu(s)]^{n+1}}.$$

2. Stationary stochastic processes. A stochastic process $\{\xi_t, \ t \in T\}$ is called stationary (in the strict sense) if the joint distribution function of the random variables $\{\xi_{t_1+\tau}, \xi_{t_2+\tau}, \dots, \xi_{t_n+\tau}\}$ is identical with the joint distribution function of the random variables $\{\xi_{t_1}, \xi_{t_2}, \dots, \xi_{t_n}\}$ for all those values of τ for which the values $t_1, t_2, \dots, t_n$ and $t_1 + \tau, t_2 + \tau, \dots, t_n + \tau$ all belong to T. A stochastic process $\{\xi_t\}$ is called *stationary in the wide sense* if $\mathbf{E}\{\xi_t\}$

and $\mathbf{E}\{\xi_t^2\}$ exist and are independent of t, and furthermore if $\mathbf{E}\{\xi_t \xi_{t+\tau}\}$ depends only on τ, where $t \in T$ and $t + \tau \in T$.

We remark that $\{\xi_t\}$ is called *homogeneous* if for all n the joint distribution of $\xi_{t_k} - \xi_{u_k}$ $(k = 1, 2, \ldots, n)$ is invariant under a translation of time.

In what follows we shall deal only with stationary processes in the wide sense, that is, we shall assume that $\{\xi_t\}$ are real random variables for $-\infty < t < \infty$, $\mathbf{E}\{\xi_t\}$ and $\mathbf{E}\{\xi_t^2\}$ exist and are independent of t, and the correlation coefficient $\mathbf{R}\{\xi_t, \xi_s\}$ of the random variables ξ_t and ξ_s depends only on $|t - s|$. Write

$$\mathbf{R}\{\xi_t, \xi_s\} = R(t - s).$$

The even function $R(t)$ is called the *correlation function* of the process.

If $R(0+) = 1$ then $R(t)$ is continuous everywhere and the stationary process $\{\xi_t\}$ is also continuous.

Theorem of Khintchine. A necessary and sufficient condition for a function $R(t)$ to be the correlation function of a continuous stationary stochastic process is that a representation of the form

$$(26) \qquad R(t) = \int_{-\infty}^{\infty} \cos tx \, dF(x)$$

exists where $F(x)$ is a probability distribution function. $F(x)$ is the *spectral distribution function* of the process.

Stochastic integrals. Let us consider a real or complex function $f(t)$ in the interval $a \le t \le b$ and a real or complex stochastic process $\{\xi(t)\}$. The *stochastic integral*

$$I = \int_a^b f(t)\xi(t) \, dt$$

is defined as a certain limit of the random variables

$$I_n = \sum_{i=1}^{n} f(t_i)\xi(t_i)(t_i - t_{i-1})$$

belonging to different partitions $a = t_0 < t_1 < \ldots < t_n = b$ when $\max_{1 \le i \le n} (t_i - t_{i-1}) \to 0$.

E

The *stochastic Stieltjes integral*

$$I^* = \int_a^b f(t)\, d\xi(t)$$

is defined as a certain limit of the random variables

$$I_n^* = \sum_{i=1}^n f(t_i)\, [\xi(t_i) - \xi(t_{i-1})],$$

belonging to different partitions $a = t_0 < t_1 < \ldots < t_n = b$, when $\max_{1 \le i \le n} (t_i - t_{i-1}) \longrightarrow 0$.

In what follows we shall concern ourselves only with convergence in mean square, namely, we shall assume that

$$\lim_{n \to \infty} \mathbf{E}\{(I_n - I)^2\} = 0 \qquad \text{and} \qquad \lim_{n \to \infty} \mathbf{E}\{(I_n^* - I^*)^2\} = 0.$$

Let us consider a stationary stochastic process $\{\xi_t\}$ for which $\mathbf{E}\{\xi_t\} = 0$, $\mathbf{E}\{\xi_t^2\} = 1$ and the correlation function is $R(t)$, then we have

$$(27) \qquad \mathbf{E}\left\{ \int_a^b f(t)\xi(t)\, dt \right\} = 0$$

and

$$(28) \qquad \mathbf{E}\left\{ \left[\int_a^b f(t)\xi(t)\, dt \right]^2 \right\} = \int_a^b \int_a^b R(t - s)f(t)f(s)\, dt\, ds,$$

if the integral exists.

Theorem of Kolmogorov and Cramér. Let there be given a stationary stochastic process $\{\xi(t)\}$ for which $\mathbf{E}\{\xi(t)\} = 0$, and $\mathbf{E}\{(\xi(t))^2\} = 1$. Then the process $\{\xi(t)\}$ can be represented as a stochastic Stieltjes integral

$$(29) \qquad \xi(t) = \int_{-\infty}^{\infty} e^{i\lambda t}\, d\zeta(\lambda),$$

where $\{\zeta(\lambda)\}$ is a complex valued stochastic process for which $\mathbf{E}\{\zeta(\lambda)\} = 0$ for all λ, and

$$\mathbf{E}\{[\zeta(\lambda_1 + \Delta\lambda_1) - \zeta(\lambda_1)]\, [\overline{\zeta(\lambda_2 + \Delta\lambda_2) - \zeta(\lambda_2)}]\} = 0$$

for disjoint intervals $(\lambda_1, \lambda_1 + \Delta\lambda_1)$ and $(\lambda_2, \lambda_2 + \Delta\lambda_2)$. (The bar is used to indicate the complex conjugate of a complex number.)

Expression (29) is called the *spectral representation* of the process $\{\xi(t)\}$. The spectral distribution function $F(x)$ of $\{\xi(t)\}$ satisfies the relation

$$(30) \qquad F(\lambda + \Delta\lambda) - F(\lambda) = \mathbf{E}\{[\zeta(\lambda + \Delta\lambda) - \zeta(\lambda)]^2\}.$$

The process $\zeta(\lambda)$ can be determined as follows:

$$\zeta(\lambda) = \frac{1}{2\pi} \lim_{T \to \infty} \int_{-T}^{T} \frac{1 - e^{i\lambda t}}{it} \xi(t)\, dt.$$

Linear prediction for stationary stochastic processes. Let us assume that the sample function of a stationary stochastic process $\{\xi(u)\}$ is known for $u \leq t$ and by the aid of this sample function we wish to predict the values $\xi(t + \tau)$ for $\tau > 0$. We want to measure the effectiveness of the prediction by measuring the mean-square error and we shall assume that the approximating value of $\xi(t + \tau)$ depends linearly on $\xi(u)$, $u \leq t$, that is, we want to determine the linear prediction

$$\xi(t + \tau) \sim L_\tau(t)$$

so that the random variable $L_\tau(t)$ shall minimize the expectation

$$(31) \qquad \mathbf{E}\{[\xi(t + \tau) - L_\tau(t)]^2\}.$$

Let us assume for the sake of simplicity that $\mathbf{E}\{\xi(t)\} = 0$ and $\mathbf{E}\{(\xi(t))^2\} = 1$, which, with a linear transformation, can always be achieved. Namely, we can consider $\{[\xi(t) - \mathbf{E}\{\xi(t)\}]/\mathbf{D}\{\xi(t)\}\}$ instead of $\{\xi(t)\}$. If

$$L_\tau(t) = \lim_{n \to \infty} \sum_{k=1}^{n} \alpha_k \xi(t - s_k),$$

then let

$$(32) \qquad \Phi_\tau(\lambda) = \lim_{n \to \infty} \sum_{k=1}^{n} \alpha_k e^{-i\lambda s_k}.$$

By means of this, on the basis of the representation (29), we can write

$$(33) \qquad L_\tau(t) = \int_{-\infty}^{\infty} e^{it\lambda} \Phi_\tau(\lambda)\, d\zeta(\lambda).$$

The function $\Phi_\tau(\lambda)$ is called the *spectral characteristic function* for the linear prediction of the process $\{\xi(t)\}$.

This function $\Phi_\tau(\lambda)$ determines uniquely the best linear prediction for $\xi(t + \tau)$. We obtain the following condition to determine $\Phi_\tau(\lambda)$

$$(34) \qquad \int_{-\infty}^{\infty} e^{is\lambda}[e^{i\tau\lambda} - \Phi_\tau(\lambda)] \, dF(\lambda) = 0 \qquad \text{if} \quad s \geqq 0.$$

The minimum of the mean-square error (31) is

$$(35) \qquad \sigma_\tau^2 = \int_{-\infty}^{\infty} [1 - |\Phi_\tau(\lambda)|^2] \, dF(\lambda).$$

If we assume that $F(\lambda)$ is absolutely continuous and the density function $f(\lambda) = F'(\lambda)$ is bounded and is a rational function of λ, then $\Phi_\tau(\lambda)$ can be determined in a simple way by applying the method of the theory of complex functions. The condition (34) is satisfied if

$1°$. $[e^{i\tau\lambda} - \Phi_\tau(\lambda)]f(\lambda)$ is a regular function of λ in the upper half plane and for $|\lambda| \to \infty$ it vanishes faster than $1/|\lambda|^{1+\varepsilon}$ where $\varepsilon > 0$.

$2°$. $\Phi_\tau(\lambda)$ is regular in the lower half plane and for $|\lambda| \to \infty$ it increases slower than a power of $|\lambda|$.

$3°$. We have

$$\int_{-\infty}^{\infty} |\Phi_\tau(\lambda)|^2 f(\lambda) \, d\lambda < \infty.$$

3. Secondary stochastic processes generated by a stochastic process. Let us consider a Poisson or recurrent stochastic process $\{\xi_t\}$ where ξ_t denotes the number of random events which occur in the time interval $(0, t]$. Suppose that each random event gives rise to a signal depending on a random parameter. Suppose that the magnitude of each signal varies according to a function $f(u, x)$, where u is the time measured from the instant of occurrence of the corresponding random event and x is the value of the corresponding random parameter. Furthermore, assume that the different signals linearly superpose, and let η_t denote the sum of the amplitudes of the signals at the instant t. The process $\{\eta_t\}$ is called a secondary stochastic process. According to what we have already said η_t can be expressed as follows:

(36) $$\eta_t = \sum_{0 < \tau_k \leq t} f(t - \tau_k, \chi_k)$$

where $\{\tau_k\}$ are the instants of occurrence of the random events taking place in the time interval $(0, t]$ and $\{\chi_k\}$ are the values of the random parameter. In what follows it will be assumed that $\{\chi_k\}$ are identically-distributed independent random variables with distribution function $H(x)$ and that the sequences $\{\chi_k\}$ and $\{\tau_k\}$ are mutually independent.

The process $\{\eta_t\}$ can also be represented in the form of a stochastic integral as follows:

$$\eta_t = \int_0^t f(t - u, \chi_u) \, d\xi_u,$$

where the random variables $\{\chi_u\}$ are independent of each other and of the process $\{\xi_u\}$ and their distribution function is $H(x)$.

Let $\mathbf{P}\{\eta_t \leq x\} = F(t, x)$. If the limiting distribution

$$\lim_{t \to \infty} \mathbf{P}\{\eta_t \leq x\} = F(x)$$

exists, and if

$$\lim_{t \to \infty} \mathbf{E}\{\eta_t\} = M, \qquad \lim_{t \to \infty} \mathbf{D}^2\{\eta\} = D^2$$

are finite, then we can define a *stationary process* $\{\eta_t^*\}$ as follows:

$$\eta_t^* = \sum_{-\infty < \tau_k \leq t} f(t - \tau_k, \chi_k)$$

where we suppose that the process $\{\tau_k\}$ starts at $t = -\infty$. It holds for the process $\{\eta_t^*\}$ that

$$\mathbf{P}\{\eta_t^* \leq x\} = F(x), \qquad \mathbf{E}\{\eta_t^*\} = M, \qquad \mathbf{D}^2\{\eta_t^*\} = D^2$$

for all t and the correlation coefficient $\mathbf{R}\{\eta_t^*, \eta_{t+\tau}^*\} = R(\tau)$ exists and depends only on τ.

Problems for solution

1. Determine the average function $m(t)$ in (2) in a direct way and show that (5) holds.

2. Show the validity of (9) making use of the following theorem of Tauberian type: If $m(t)$ is a monotone non-decreasing function, if

$$\mu(s) = \int_0^\infty e^{-st} \, dm(t)$$

exists for $\Re(s) > 0$ and $\lim_{s \to 0} s\mu(s) = C$, then $\lim_{t \to \infty} m(t)/t = C$.

3. Let $\{\xi_t\}$ be a recurrent stochastic process. Prove that if $\sigma^2 < \infty$, then the distribution of ξ_t is asymptotically normal, that is,

$$\lim_{t \to \infty} \mathbf{P}\left\{ \frac{\xi_t - t/\mu}{\sqrt{\sigma^2 t/\mu^3}} \leq x \right\} = \frac{1}{\sqrt{2\pi}} \int_{-\infty}^x e^{-u^2/2} du.$$

4. Let $\{\xi_t\}$ be a recurrent stochastic process. Prove that if $F(x)$ is not a lattice distribution function and if $\mu < \infty$, then

$$\lim_{u \to \infty} \mathbf{P}\{\xi_{u+t} - \xi_u \leq n\} = W^*(t, n),$$

where $W^*(t, n)$ is defined by (18).

5. Consider a recurrent process $\{\xi_t\}$. Let us select a random point distributed uniformly on the interval $(0, t]$ and denote by η_t^* its distance from the next random event. Determine $\mathbf{P}\{\eta_t^* \leq x\}$ and prove that if $\mu < \infty$, then

$$\lim_{t \to \infty} \mathbf{P}\{\eta_t^* \leq x\} = F^*(x)$$

where $F^*(x)$ is defined by (15).

6. Consider a recurrent process $\{\xi_t\}$. Let us choose a random point τ distributed uniformly on the interval $(0, T]$ and determine the limiting distribution of the random variable $\xi_{\tau+t} - \xi_\tau$ as $T \to \infty$. Show that if $\mu < \infty$, then

$$\lim_{T \to \infty} \mathbf{P}\{\xi_{\tau+t} - \xi_\tau \leq n\} = W^*(t, n)$$

where $W^*(t, n)$ is defined by (18).

7. Show that if $F(x)$ is not a lattice distribution function and if $\sigma^2 < \infty$, then

$$\lim_{t \to \infty} \left[m(t) - \frac{t}{\mu} \right] = \frac{\sigma^2}{2\mu^2} - \frac{1}{2}.$$

8. Consider a recurrent process $\{\xi_t\}$. Suppose that $F(x)$ is not lattice distribution function. Let $\nu = \xi_t$ and determine the limiting distribution of the random variable $\vartheta_t = \tau_{\nu+1} - \tau_\nu$ for $t \to \infty$.

9. *Renewal theory.* Let us suppose that

$$f(x) = e^{-\lambda x} \frac{(\lambda x)^{m-1}}{(m-1)!} \lambda$$

is the lifetime density function of a part of a continuously working machine. At $t = 0$ we place such a part in the machine. If it breaks down we replace it promptly. What is the expectation of the number of replacements in the time interval $(0, t]$.

10. Let us consider a general recurrent process such as we considered in Section 1; assume that the distribution function of the random variable τ_1 is $\hat{F}(x)$, and let $\hat{\phi}(s) = \int_0^\infty e^{-sx} d\hat{F}(x)$ be its Laplace–Stieltjes transform. Determine $\mathbf{P}\{\xi_t \leq n\}$, $m(t) = \mathbf{E}\{\xi_t\}$ and the Laplace–Stieltjes transform of $m(t)$.

11. An electron multiplier is used for counting particles which arrive according to a Poisson process with density λ. Each particle gives rise to an impulse of duration α in the multiplier. However, only those particles will be registered which arrive at an instant when there is no impulse present. Determine the distribution of the number of registered particles in the time interval $(0, t]$, and its asymptotic distribution as $t \to \infty$.

12. A Geiger–Müller counter tube is used for recording particles which arrive according to a Poisson process of density λ. The first particle gives rise to an impulse of duration α. The other particles give rise to an impulse of the duration α if and only if at this instant there is no impulse present. Particles which arrive during the dead time—that is when there is an impulse present—are not registered. Determine the distribution of the number of registered particles in the time interval $(0, t]$ and its asymptotic distribution as $t \to \infty$.

13. We are counting particles arriving according to a Poisson process of density λ with a counter tube which produces an impulse of duration α for each particle which arrives when there is no impulse present. Those particles which arrive when there is an impulse present produce impulses of duration α with probability p

independently of each other. But only those particles are registered which arrive when there is no impulse present. Determine the asymptotic distribution of the registered particles in the time interval $(0, t]$ as $t \longrightarrow \infty$ and the density of the registered particles.

14. Consider Problem 11 with the modification that the durations of impulses are identically-distributed, independent random variables with distribution function $H(x)$. Let

$$\alpha = \int_0^\infty x \, dH(x).$$

15. Consider Problem 12 with the modification that the durations of impulses are identically-distributed random variables with distribution function $H(x)$. Let

$$\alpha = \int_0^\infty x \, dH(x), \qquad \beta^2 = \int_0^\infty (x - \alpha)^2 \, dH(x).$$

16. *Successive transformation.* Assume that impulses are produced by a counter according to a recurrent process. However, not all impulses are recorded, because the amplifier has a dead time τ and no new impulse is recorded during time τ after one has been recorded. Determine the density of recorded impulses.

17. Apply the result of Problem 16 to Problem 11.

18. Apply the result of Problem 16 to Problem 12.

19. *Random coincidence.* Suppose that m Geiger–Müller counters are used for counting particles which arrive according to m independent Poisson processes of density λ. Assume that $H(x) = 1 - e^{-x/\alpha}$ $(x \geq 0)$ is the distribution function of the length of impulses started by the particles in each counter. The system is said to be in the state E_j $(j = 0, 1, \ldots, m)$ at a given instant if j impulses are in progress at this instant. The transition $E_{j-1} \longrightarrow E_j$ is called a j-fold chance coincidence. Determine the density of m-fold chance coincidences and the asymptotic distribution of the m-fold chance coincidences occurring in the time interval $(0, t]$ as $t \longrightarrow \infty$.

20. *Random scaling.* Suppose that impulses are arriving at a scaler according to a recurrent process and that only the $\nu_1, \nu_1 + \nu_2, \ldots, \nu_1 + \nu_2 + \ldots + \nu_n, \ldots$ impulses are let through by the scaler where $\{\nu_n\}$ are identically distributed, independent, random variables with mean value $E\{v_n\} = a$ and variance $D^2\{v_n\} = b^2$. Determine the asymptotic distribution of the number of registered impulses during the time interval $(0, t]$ as $t \rightarrow \infty$.

21. Let $R(t) = e^{-\alpha|t|}$ be the correlation function of a stationary stochastic process $\{\xi_t\}$. Determine the spectral distribution function $F(x)$.

22. Show that the correlation function $R(t)$ of a stationary stochastic process $\{\xi_t\}$ is continuous if $R(0 +) = 1$.

23. Let $\xi_t = \xi \cos \alpha t + \eta \sin at$, where ξ and η are uncorrelated random variables for which $E\{\xi\} = E\{\eta\} = 0$ and $E\{\xi^2\} = E\{\eta^2\} = 1$. Show that $\{\xi_t\}$ is a stationary stochastic process and determine its correlation function $R(t)$ and its spectral distribution function $F(x)$.

24. Let $\xi(t)$ be a stationary stochastic process with $E\{\xi(t)\} = 0$, $D\{\xi(t)\} = 1$ and $R(t) = e^{-\alpha|t|}$, where $\alpha > 0$. Determine the linear prediction for $\xi(t + \tau)$ by the principle of least squares, using the sample values $\xi(s)$, $(s \le t)$ only.

25. Let $\xi(t)$ be a stationary stochastic process with $E\{\xi(t)\} = 0$ and $D\{\xi(t)\} = 1$. Let

$$f(\lambda) = \frac{C}{\lambda^4 + \alpha^4}$$

be its spectral density function, where $\alpha > 0$. Determine the linear prediction for $\xi(t + \tau)$ on the basis of the principle of least-squares using the values $\xi(s)$, $s \le t$ only.

26. Let

$$f(\lambda) = C\frac{\lambda^2 + \alpha^2}{\lambda^4 + \alpha^4}$$

be the spectral density function of a stationary stochastic process $\{\xi_t\}$. Determine the linear prediction for $\xi(t + \tau)$ on the basis of the principle of least squares using the values $\xi(s)$, $s \le t$ only.

27. *Shot-noise.* It is assumed that the electron emission from the cathode of an electron tube follows a Poisson process of density λ. The electrons while flying from cathode to anode induce a current impulse in the anode circuit of the tube. Let the intensity of the current created by an electron be $f(u, x)$, where u is the time of flight of the electron and x is the velocity of the emitted electron. Let $H(x)$ be the distribution function of the initial velocity of emitted electrons. The anode current is the linear superposition of the elementary current impulses created by single electrons. Determine in the stationary case the distribution of anode current η_t^*, its mean value and its variance.

28. Determine in Problem 27 the correlation function of the process $\{\eta_t^*\}$ and the spectral distribution of the current.

29. Determine in Problem 27 the mean value and the variance of the average current

$$\frac{1}{T} \int_0^T \eta_t^* dt.$$

30. Consider a plane diode the cathode of which emits electrons according to a Poisson process with density λ and zero initial velocity. Disregard the existence of a space charge. In this case the intensity of a current impulse induced by a single electron is $f(u) = 2\varepsilon u/\tau_0^2$ if $0 \leq u \leq \tau_0$, where τ_0 is the transit time and ε is the charge of an electron. Determine the distribution function, variance, correlation function and spectral distribution of the anode current η_t^*.

31. Determine in Problem 30 the variance of the average current

$$\frac{1}{T} \int_0^T \eta_t^* dt.$$

32. Consider Problem 31 of Chapter 2. Determine $\mathbf{P}\{\xi_t \leq x\} = F(t, x)$ and

$$\lim_{t \to \infty} \mathbf{P}\{\xi_t \leq x\} = F(x).$$

Let us suppose now that a particle is registered only if the voltage on the input resistance of the amplifier exceeds a threshold value a. Determine the density of registrations. Consider the special case when the amplitudes of the impulses are equal to a constant μ.

33. Consider Problem 21 of Chapter 1. Assume that particles are registered only if the voltage on the input resistance exceeds a threshold value a. Determine the density of registrations in the stationary case.

CHAPTER 4

SOLUTIONS OF PROBLEMS

1. Markov chains

1. The proof may be accomplished by induction. Use the following form of the theorem of total probability:

$$\mathbf{P}\{A \mid C\} = \sum_{j=1}^{\infty} \mathbf{P}\{B_j \mid C\}\mathbf{P}\{A \mid B_jC\},$$

where $\{B_j\}$ is a complete system of events and $\mathbf{P}\{C\} > 0$.

2. Use the above formula in which now event A denotes that $\xi_n = k$, event B denotes that $\xi_1 = j$ and event C denotes that $\xi_0 = i$.

3. From equation (15) we obtain

$$f_j = \left\{\sum_{n=1}^{\infty} p_{jj}^{(n)}\right\} \bigg/ \left\{1 + \sum_{n=1}^{\infty} p_{jj}^{(n)}\right\}.$$

If $\sum_{n=1}^{\infty} p_{jj}^{(n)} = \infty$, then $f_j = 1$ and conversely, and in this case E_j is a recurrent state.

If $\sum_{n=1}^{\infty} p_{jj}^{(n)} < \infty$, then $f_j < 1$ and conversely, and in this case E is a transient state.

4. We have the following relation amongst the generating functions: $F_j(z) + F_j(z)P_j(z) = P_j(z)$.

5. The matrix of the transition probabilities is

$$\pi = \left\|\begin{matrix} p & q \\ q & p \end{matrix}\right\|.$$

Its eigenvalues are $\lambda_1 = 1$ and $\lambda_2 = p - q$ and according to (12)

$$\pi^n = \frac{1}{2} \begin{Vmatrix} 1 & 1 \\ 1 & 1 \end{Vmatrix} + \frac{(p-q)^n}{2} \begin{Vmatrix} 1 & -1 \\ -1 & 1 \end{Vmatrix}.$$

Whence

$$P_1(n) = \alpha p_{11}^{(n)} + \beta p_{21}^{(n)} = \frac{1}{2} + \frac{(\alpha - \beta)(p - q)^n}{2}$$

and

$$P_2(n) = \alpha p_{12}^{(n)} + \beta p_{22}^{(n)} = \frac{1}{2} - \frac{(\alpha - \beta)(p - q)^n}{2}.$$

Furthermore,

$$\lim_{n \to \infty} P_1(n) = \lim_{n \to \infty} P_2(n) = \frac{1}{2}.$$

The Markov chain in question is ergodic and its limiting distribution (P_1, P_2) can be obtained also by solving the following system of equations

$$P_1 = P_1 p + P_2 q$$
$$P_2 = P_1 q + P_2 p$$
$$P_1 + P_2 = 1,$$

6. We have

$$\mathbf{P}\{\xi_0 = i \mid \xi_n = j\} = \frac{\mathbf{P}\{\xi_0 = i\}\mathbf{P}\{\xi_n = j \mid \xi_0 = i\}}{\mathbf{P}\{\xi_n = j\}} = \frac{P_i(0)p_{ij}^{(n)}}{P_j(n)}.$$

7. We have

$$\mathbf{P}\{\xi_0 = 1 \mid \xi_n = 1\} = \frac{\alpha p_{11}^{(n)}}{P_1(n)} = \frac{\alpha + \alpha(p - q)^n}{1 + (\alpha - \beta)(p - q)^n}.$$

8. The first chain is irreducible and aperiodic. The second chain is irreducible and periodic with period $t = 3$ and with the following sub-sets of states $G_1 = \{E_1\}$, $G_2 = \{E_2\}$, $G_3 = \{E_3, E_4\}$. The third chain has two aperiodic closed sets, $\{E_1, E_2\}$ and $\{E_3, E_4\}$ and a transient state E_5.

9. It is known in the theory of cyclic determinants that

$$|\boldsymbol{\pi} - \lambda \mathbf{I}| = \prod_{j=1}^{m} [\phi(\varepsilon_j) - \lambda], \text{ where } \phi(\varepsilon) = p_0 + p_1\varepsilon + \ldots + p_{m-1}\varepsilon^{m-1}$$

and $\varepsilon_j = e^{\frac{2\pi i(j-1)}{m}}$ $(j = 1, 2, \ldots, m)$ are the m-th roots of unity.

Here $i = \sqrt{-1}$. The eigenvalues of π are thus

$$\lambda_j = \phi(\varepsilon_j) = p_0 + p_1\varepsilon_j + \ldots + p_{m-1}\varepsilon_j^{m-1} \; (j = 1, 2, \ldots, m).$$

Now if $\mathbf{A} = \| \alpha_{ij} \|$, where $\alpha_{ij} = \varepsilon_j^{i-1}$ and $\mathbf{B} = \| \beta_{jk} \|$ where $\beta_{jk} = \varepsilon_j^{-(k-1)}$ $(i, j, k = 1, 2, \ldots, m)$, then $\pi\mathbf{A} = \mathbf{A}\Lambda$ and $\mathbf{A}\mathbf{B} = m\mathbf{I}$, where Λ is a diagonal matrix consisting of the eigenvalues $\lambda_1, \lambda_2, \ldots, \lambda_m$. Thus

$$\pi = \frac{1}{m}\mathbf{A}\Lambda\mathbf{B}$$

and consequently

$$\pi^n = \frac{1}{m}\mathbf{A}\Lambda^n\mathbf{B}.$$

Since

$$\lim_{n \to \infty} \Lambda^n = \lim_{n \to \infty} \begin{Vmatrix} \lambda_1^n & 0 & \ldots & 0 \\ 0 & \lambda_2^n & \ldots & 0 \\ . & . & \ldots & . \\ 0 & 0 & \ldots & \lambda_m^n \end{Vmatrix} = \begin{Vmatrix} 1 & 0 & \ldots & 0 \\ 0 & 0 & \ldots & 0 \\ . & . & \ldots & . \\ 0 & 0 & \ldots & 0 \end{Vmatrix},$$

we have

$$\lim_{n \to \infty} \pi^n = \frac{1}{m} \begin{Vmatrix} 1 & 1 & \ldots & 1 \\ 1 & 1 & \ldots & 1 \\ . & . & \ldots & . \\ 1 & 1 & \ldots & 1 \end{Vmatrix},$$

which was to be proved. The Markov chain in question is irreducible and ergodic and its limiting distribution $\{P_j\}$ $(P_j = 1/m, \; j = 1, 2, \ldots, m)$ can also be directly determined by Theorem 2.

10. The transition probabilities are

$$p_{jj} = \frac{2j(N-j)}{N^2}, \quad p_{j,j+1} = \frac{(N-j)^2}{N^2}, \quad p_{j,j-1} = \frac{j^2}{N^2},$$
$$(j = 0, 1, \ldots, N).$$

The Markov chain in question consists of a finite number of states, it is irreducible and aperiodic and therefore according to Markov's theorem there exists a unique limiting distribution $\{P_j\}$ which can be determined by solving the following system of linear equations:

$$\begin{cases} P_j = P_{j-1}p_{j-1,j} + P_j p_{jj} + P_{j+1}p_{j+1,j} \quad (j = 0, 1, \ldots, N) \\ \sum_{j=0}^{N} P_j = 1. \end{cases}$$

The solution is

$$P_j = \binom{N}{j}^2 \Big/ \binom{2N}{N}, \qquad (j = 0, 1, \ldots, N).$$

11. This chain is irreducible and has period $t = 2$.

In order to obtain the transition probabilities $p_{ik}^{(n)}$, let us form the canonical form of the matrix $\| p_{ik} \|$. First consider the equation

$$y'\pi = \lambda y',$$

where π is the matrix of transition probabilities and

$$y' = \| \beta_0, \beta_1, \ldots, \beta_a \|.$$

Writing these equations in detail we have

$$\frac{a-k+1}{a}\beta_{k-1} + \frac{k+1}{a}\beta_{k+1} = \lambda\beta_k, \qquad (k = 0, 1, \ldots, a),$$

where $\beta_{a+1} = \beta_{-1} = 0$. Let us introduce the generating function

$$U(z) = \beta_0 + \beta_1 z + \ldots + \beta_a z^a.$$

For this we have

$$(1 - z^2)U'(z) + a(z - \lambda)U(z) = 0,$$

whence

$$U(z) = A(1 - z)^{\frac{a(1-\lambda)}{2}}(1 + z)^{\frac{a(1+\lambda)}{2}},$$

where A is a constant. Since $U(z)$ is a polynomial of degree a, therefore we must have $\lambda = 1 - 2j/a$ $(j = 0, 1, \ldots, a)$. The numbers $\lambda_j = 1 - 2j/a$ $(j = 0, 1, \ldots, a)$ are the eigenvalues of π. Let $y_j' = \| \beta_{j0}, \beta_{j1}, \ldots, \beta_{ja} \|$ be the left eigenvector belonging to λ_j. Then

$$\sum_{k=0}^{a} \beta_{jk} z^k = A_j(1 - z)^j(1 + z)^{a-j},$$

where A_j is an arbitrary constant for which a suitable value will be chosen later. If the right eigenvector belonging to λ_j is

$$\mathbf{x}_j = \begin{Vmatrix} \alpha_{0j} \\ \alpha_{1j} \\ \cdot \\ \cdot \\ \cdot \\ \alpha_{aj} \end{Vmatrix},$$

and $\mathbf{x}_j$ is normalized so that $\mathbf{y}_j'\mathbf{x}_j = 1$ $(j = 0, 1, \ldots, a)$, then we may write

$$z^i = \sum_{k=0}^{a} \delta_{ik}z^k = \sum_{k=0}^{a} z^k \sum_{j=0}^{a} \alpha_{ij}\beta_{jk} = \sum_{j=0}^{a} \alpha_{ij}A_j(1-z)^j(1+z)^{a-}$$

$$= (1+z)^a \sum_{j=0}^{a} \alpha_{ij} A_j \left(\frac{1-z}{1+z}\right)^j.$$

By substituting $\zeta = (1-z)/(1+z)$ we obtain

$$\sum_{j=0}^{a} \alpha_{ij}A_j\zeta^j = \frac{(1-\zeta)^i(1+\zeta)^{a-i}}{2^a}.$$

Let, now, $A_j = 1/2^{a/2}$. This readily shows that the two matrices $\|\alpha_{ij}\|$ and $\|\beta_{jk}\|$ coincide while they are inverse matrices. Accordingly, if $\mathbf{H} = \|\alpha_{ij}\|$ we may write

$$\boldsymbol{\pi} = \mathbf{H}\boldsymbol{\Lambda}\mathbf{H},$$

where

$$\sum_{j=0}^{a} \alpha_{ij}z^j = \frac{(1-z)^i(1+z)^{a-i}}{2^{a/2}}$$

and $\boldsymbol{\Lambda}$ is a diagonal matrix with elements $\lambda_j = 1 - 2j/a$, $(j = 0, 1, \ldots, a)$.

Finally the transition probabilities $p_{ik}^{(n)}$ can be obtained as the elements of the matrix

$$\boldsymbol{\pi}^n = \mathbf{H}\boldsymbol{\Lambda}^n\mathbf{H}.$$

The stationary distribution can be directly determined as the solution of the equations

$$\begin{cases} P_j^* = \left(1 - \frac{j-1}{a}\right)P_{j-1}^* + \frac{j+1}{a}P_{j+1}^*, & (j = 1, 2, \ldots, a-1), \\ P_0^* = \frac{1}{a}P_1^*, \qquad P_a^* = \frac{1}{a}P_{a-1}^*. \\ \sum_{j=0}^{a} P_j^* = 1. \end{cases}$$

It can easily be proved that

$$P_j^* = \binom{a}{j}\frac{1}{2^a}, \qquad (j = 0, 1, \ldots, a).$$

12. Now $P_k(n) = p_{ik}^{(n)}$. Consider the matrix π^* with $a - 1$ rows and $a - 1$ columns

$$\pi^* = \begin{Vmatrix} 0 & p & 0 & \ldots & 0 & 0 \\ q & 0 & p & \ldots & 0 & 0 \\ . & . & . & \ldots & . & . \\ 0 & 0 & 0 & \ldots & 0 & p \\ 0 & 0 & 0 & \ldots & q & 0 \end{Vmatrix}$$

which is obtained from the matrix of transition probabilities π by omitting the first and last rows and the first and last columns. In this case the transition probabilities $p_{ik}^{(n)}$, $(1 \le i, k \le a - 1)$ will be the elements of the matrix $(\pi^*)^n$. Let us find the canonical form of π^*. To achieve this, consider the equation $\mathbf{y}'\pi^* = \lambda\mathbf{y}'$, where $\mathbf{y}' = \| \beta_1, \beta_2, \ldots, \beta_{a-1} \|$. Writing in the details, we have

$$p\beta_{k-1} + q\beta_{k+1} = \lambda\beta_k, \qquad (k = 1, 2, \ldots, a - 1),$$

where $\beta_a = \beta_0 = 0$. The solution of this is $\beta_k = A\omega_1^k + B\omega_2^k$, where ω_1 and ω_2 are the roots of the equation $q\omega^2 - \lambda\omega + p = 0$ (as it is known $q\omega_1\omega_2 = p$ and $\lambda = q(\omega_1 + \omega_2)$). Owing to conditions $\beta_0 = 0$ and $\beta_a = 0$ we have $A + B = 0$ and $\omega_1^a = \omega_2^a$, that is,

$$\omega_1 = \omega_2 e^{\frac{2\pi ij}{a}} \ (j = 1, 2, \ldots, a - 1),$$

where $i = \sqrt{-1}$, and since $\omega_1\omega_2 = p/q$ it follows that

$$\omega_1 = \sqrt{\frac{p}{q}} e^{\frac{\pi ij}{a}}, \omega_2 = \sqrt{\frac{p}{q}} e^{-\frac{\pi ij}{a}} \qquad (j = 1, 2, \ldots, a - 1)$$

and the eigenvalues of π^* are

$$\lambda = q(\omega_1 + \omega_2) = 2\sqrt{pq}\cos\frac{\pi j}{a}, \qquad (j = 1, 2, \ldots, a-1).$$

Thus

$$\beta_k = \beta_{kj} = A_j\left(\frac{p}{q}\right)^{k/2}\sin\frac{\pi jk}{a}, \qquad (k = 1, 2, \ldots, a-1),$$

will be the solution which belongs to the eigenvalue

$$\lambda_j = 2\sqrt{pq}\cos\frac{\pi j}{a} \qquad (j = 1, 2, \ldots, a-1).$$

We obtain similarly that the solution of $\pi^*\mathbf{x}_j = \lambda_j\mathbf{x}_j$ $(j = 1, 2, \ldots, a-1)$ is

$$\mathbf{x} = \left\| \begin{array}{c} \alpha_{1j} \\ \alpha_{2j} \\ \cdot \\ \cdot \\ \cdot \\ \alpha_{a-1,j} \end{array} \right\|,$$

where

$$\alpha_{ij} = B\left(\frac{q}{p}\right)^{i/2}\sin\frac{\pi ij}{a} \qquad (i = 1, 2, \ldots, a-1).$$

Now we have

$$\frac{1}{C^j} = \sum_{v=1}^{a-1}\beta_{jv}\alpha_v = A_jB_j\sum_{v=1}^{a-1}\sin\frac{\pi jv}{a}\sin\frac{\pi vj}{a} = A_jB_j\frac{a}{2}$$

and therefore it follows from (10) that

$$p_{ik}^{(n)} = \frac{2^{n+1}p^{\frac{n+k-i}{2}}q^{\frac{n-k+i}{2}}}{a}\sum_{j=1}^{a-1}\left(\cos\frac{\pi j}{a}\right)^n\sin\frac{\pi ij}{a}\sin\frac{\pi jk}{a}$$

is the required solution.

In order to determine the absorption probabilities π^* let $C = \{E_0\}$ and $T = \{E_1, E_2, \ldots, E_{a-1}\}$. According to (22) it holds that

$$\begin{cases} \pi_1^* = p\pi_2^* + q \\ \pi_j^* = q\pi_{j-1}^* + p\pi_{j+1}^*, \qquad (j = 2, 3, \ldots, a-2), \\ \pi_{a-1}^* = q\pi_{a-2}^* \end{cases}$$

from which it follows that

$$\pi^* = \frac{\left(\frac{q}{p}\right)^a - \left(\frac{q}{p}\right)^j}{\left(\frac{q}{p}\right)^a - 1}, \qquad (j = 1, 2, \ldots, a-1),$$

if $p \neq q$ and $\pi_j^* = 1 - j/a$ if $p = q = \frac{1}{2}$.

13. The Markov chain in question is ergodic and the distribution $\{P_j\}$ will be the solution of the following system of linear equations

$$\begin{cases} qP_1 + qP_2 = P_1 \\ pP_{j-1} + qP_{j+1} = P_j, & (j = 2, 3, \ldots, a-1) \\ pP_{a-1} + pP_a = P_a. \end{cases}$$

Now $P_j = \frac{p}{q} P_{j-1}$, whence $P_j = \left(\frac{p}{q}\right)^{j-1} P_1$, $(j = 1, 2, \ldots, a)$. P_1 is determined from the condition $\sum_{j=1}^{a} P_j = 1$. Thus we have finally that

$$P_j = \frac{1 - \frac{p}{q}}{1 - \left(\frac{p}{q}\right)^a} \left(\frac{p}{q}\right)^{j-1}, \qquad (j = 1, 2, \ldots, a),$$

if $p \neq q$ and $P_j = 1/a$ $(j = 1, 2, \ldots, a)$ if $p = q = \frac{1}{2}$.

The transition probabilities $p_{ik}^{(n)}$ can be determined in the same way as in Problem 12. Now the eigenvalues of π are

$$\lambda_j = 2(pq)^{1/2} \cos \frac{\pi j}{a}, \; (j = 1, 2, \ldots, a-1), \text{ and } \lambda_0 = 1,$$

and the elements of the matrices $\| \alpha_{ij} \|$ and $\| \beta_{jk} \|$, which are built up from the left and right eigenvectors respectively, are

$$\alpha_{ij} = \left(\frac{q}{p}\right)^{i/2} \sin \frac{\pi i j}{a} - \left(\frac{q}{p}\right)^{\frac{i+1}{2}} \sin \frac{\pi(i-1)j}{a},$$
$$(j = 1, 2, \ldots, a-1),$$

and $\alpha_{i0} = 1$, and

$$\beta_{jk} = \left(\frac{p}{q}\right)^{k/2} \sin\frac{\pi jk}{a} - \left(\frac{p}{q}\right)^{\frac{k-1}{2}} \sin\frac{\pi j(k-1)}{a},$$

$$(j = 1, 2, \ldots, a-1),$$

and $\beta_{k0} = \left(\frac{p}{q}\right)^k$.

It follows from (10) that

$$p_{ik}^{(n)} = \sum_{j=0}^{a-1} C_j \lambda_j^n \alpha_{ij} \beta_{jk},$$

where

$$C_j = \frac{2p}{a\left[1 - 2(pq)^{1/2}\cos\dfrac{\pi j}{a}\right]}, \quad (j = 1, 2, \ldots, a-1),$$

and

$$C_0 = \begin{cases} \dfrac{q}{p}\, \dfrac{1 - \dfrac{p}{q}}{1 - \left(\dfrac{p}{q}\right)^a} & \text{if} \quad p \neq q \\[4mm] \dfrac{1}{a} & \text{if} \quad p = q. \end{cases}$$

14. The Markov chain in question is irreducible, aperiodic and also ergodic if $\lambda\alpha < 1$. If $\lambda\alpha \geqq 1$, then the states are recurrent null ($\lambda\alpha = 1$) or transient ($\lambda\alpha > 1$). For, denote by μ_0 the mean recurrence time of the state E_0. Then it is easy to see that

$$\mu_0\frac{1}{\lambda} = \mu_0\alpha + \frac{1}{\lambda}$$

and consequently $\mu_0 = 1/(1 - \lambda\alpha) < \infty$ if $\lambda\alpha < 1$ and $\mu_0 = \infty$ if $\lambda\alpha \geqq 1$. That is, $P_0 > 0$ if $\lambda\alpha < 1$ and $P_0 = 0$ if $\lambda\alpha \geqq 1$. The limiting distribution $\{P_j\}$ satisfies the following system of linear equations:

$$P_j = P_{j+1}\pi_0 + P_j\pi_1 + \ldots + P_1\pi_j + P_0\pi_j, \quad (j = 0, 1, 2, \ldots).$$

Let

$$\Pi(z) = \sum_{j=0}^{\infty} P_j z^j$$

and

$$\pi(z) = \sum_{j=0}^{\infty} \pi_j z^j = \int_0^{\infty} e^{-\lambda(1-z)x} \, dH(x) = \psi[\lambda(1-z)],$$

where

$$\psi(s) = \int_0^{\infty} e^{-sx} \, dH(x)$$

is the Laplace–Stieltjes transform of the distribution function $H(x)$. We have for the generating functions

$$z\Pi(z) = \pi(z)[\Pi(z) + P_0 z - P_0]$$

and therefore

$$\Pi(z) = P_0 \frac{\pi(z)}{1 - \dfrac{1 - \pi(z)}{1 - z}}.$$

Now

$$\lim_{z \to 1} \frac{1 - \pi(z)}{1 - z} = \lambda \alpha$$

and consequently

$$\Pi(1) = \frac{P_0}{1 - \lambda \alpha}.$$

Now if $\lambda \alpha < 1$, then the Markov chain is ergodic and $\Pi(1) = 1$ implies that $P_0 = 1 - \lambda \alpha$. Thus

$$\Pi(z) = \frac{(1 - \lambda \alpha)\pi(z)}{1 - \dfrac{1 - \pi(z)}{1 - z}}.$$

If $\lambda \alpha \geq 1$, then the system is not ergodic and $\lim_{n \to \infty} P_j(n) = 0$ for all j.

If in the above problem we suppose specifically that

$$H(x) = 1 - e^{-x/\alpha} \text{ for } x \geq 0,$$

then $\psi(s) = 1/(1 + s\alpha)$ and in the case $\lambda \alpha < 1$ we have

$$\Pi(z) = \frac{1 - \lambda \alpha}{1 - \lambda \alpha z},$$

from which it follows that

$$P_j = (1 - \lambda\alpha)(\lambda\alpha)^j, \qquad (j = 0, 1, 2, \ldots).$$

15. In this problem the Markov chain is irreducible, aperiodic and also ergodic since the number of states is finite. The limiting probabilities P_j $(j = 0, 1, \ldots, m)$ satisfy the following system of linear equations

$$P_k = \sum_{j=k-1}^{m} p_{jk}P_j, \qquad (k = 0, 1, \ldots, m - 1),$$

and

$$\sum_{k=0}^{m} P_k = 1.$$

To solve this system of equations let us introduce the generating function

$$U(z) = \sum_{k=0}^{m} P_k z^k.$$

We obtain for $U(z)$ the following relation

$$U(z) = \int_0^\infty (1 - e^{-\mu x} + ze^{-\mu x})U(1 - e^{-\mu x} + ze^{-\mu x})\,dF(x)$$

$$+ (1 - z)P_m \int_0^\infty e^{-\mu x}(1 - e^{-\mu x} + ze^{-\mu x})^m\,dF(x).$$

Let now

$$U_r = \frac{1}{r!}\left(\frac{d^r U(z)}{dz^r}\right)_{z=1}$$

and

$$\phi_r = \int_0^\infty e^{-r\mu x}\,dF(x), \qquad (r = 0, 1, 2, \ldots).$$

By differentiating the equation for $U(z)$ r-times and putting $z = 1$ we obtain

$$U_r = \frac{\phi_r}{1 - \phi_r}\left[U_{r-1} - \binom{m}{r-1}U_m\right], \qquad (r = 1, 2, \ldots, m),$$

with $P_m = U_m$. Furthermore, $U_0 = 1$. If now U_m is to be considered fixed, then the formula above furnishes a recursive equation for U_r which can easily be solved.† The solution is

$$U_r = C_r \left[1 - U_m \sum_{j=0}^{r-1} \binom{m}{j} \frac{1}{C_j} \right],$$

where

$$C_0 = 1$$

and

$$C_j = \prod_{\nu=1}^{j} \left(\frac{\phi_\nu}{1 - \phi_\nu} \right) \qquad (j = 1, 2, \ldots).$$

Now if we put $r = m$ in the formula for U_r, we obtain

$$U_m = 1 \bigg/ \sum_{j=0}^{m} \binom{m}{j} \frac{1}{C}$$

and thus

$$U_r = C_r \sum_{j=r}^{m} \binom{m}{j} \frac{1}{C_j} \bigg/ \sum_{j=0}^{m} \binom{m}{j} \frac{1}{C_j}.$$

Finally, since

$$P_k = \frac{1}{k!} \left(\frac{d^k U(z)}{dz^k} \right)_{z=0} = \sum_{r=k}^{m} (-1)^{r-k} \binom{r}{k} \frac{1}{r!} \left(\frac{d^r U(z)}{dz^r} \right)_{z=1},$$

we find

$$P_k = \sum_{r=k}^{m} (-1)^{r-k} \binom{r}{k} C_r \sum_{j=r}^{m} \binom{m}{j} \frac{1}{C_j} \bigg/ \sum_{j=0}^{m} \binom{m}{j} \frac{1}{C_j},$$
$$(k = 0, 1, \ldots, m).$$

If, in particular,

$$F(x) = \begin{cases} 1 - e^{-\lambda x} & \text{if } x \geqq 0, \\ 0 & \text{if } x < 0, \end{cases}$$

then

$$\phi_j = \frac{\lambda}{\lambda + j\mu} \quad \text{and} \quad C_j = \frac{(\lambda/\mu)^j}{j!},$$

† Cf. for example Ch. Jordan, *Calculus of Finite Differences* (Budapest, 1939; New York, 1947), p. 583.

whence

$$P_k = \frac{(\lambda/\mu)^k}{k!} \Big/ \sum_{j=0}^{m} \frac{(\lambda/\mu)^j}{j!} \qquad (k = 1, 2, \ldots, m).$$

16. The Markov chain in question is irreducible and aperiodic, and it is also ergodic if the system of linear equations (28) has a non-vanishing solution which forms an absolutely convergent series. Let $\pi_\nu = \binom{m}{\nu} p^\nu q^{m-\nu}$ (where $q = 1 - p$). Then $p_{ij} = \pi_{j-i+k}$ if $i \geq k$ and $p_{ij} = \pi_{j-i}$ if $i < k$. According to equation (28) we have

$$P_j = \sum_{i=0}^{k-1} P_i \, \pi_{j-i} + \sum_{i=k}^{\infty} P_i \pi_{j-i+k}, \qquad (j = 0, 1, 2, \ldots).$$

Let us introduce the generating function

$$U(z) = \sum_{j=0}^{\infty} P_j z^j$$

and let

$$U_k(z) = \sum_{=0}^{k-1} P_j z^j.$$

We obtain for $U(z)$ the following relation

$$U(z) = \frac{U_k(z)(z^k - 1)[1 + p(z - 1)]^m}{z^k - [1 + p(z - 1)]^m}.$$

Apparently this equation does not determine the probabilities P. since it may be thought that the polynomial $U_k(z)$ of degree $k - 1$ can be chosen arbitrarily. However, this is not the case because only for one polynomial will $\{P_j\}$ form a probability distribution. First of all it follows from the condition $U(1) = 1$ that

$$1 = U_k(1) \frac{k}{k - mp}.$$

This shows at once that the system will not be ergodic if $k \leq mp$. So in this case $\lim_{n \to \infty} P_j(n) = 0$ for all j. If, however, $mp < k$, then we shall show that $U(z)$ is uniquely determined and that the system is ergodic. This can be seen as follows. The radius of convergence of the power series for $U(z)$ is at least 1 and thus $U(z)$ is regular in the unit circle $|z| < 1$ of the complex plane. On the other hand, it follows from the theorem of Rouché that the equation $z^k - [1 + p(z - 1)]^m = 0$ has exactly $k - 1$ roots in the interior of the unit circle. Let these roots be $z_1, z_2, \ldots, z_{k-1}$. Since $U(z)$ is regular, this can happen only if $z_1, z_2, \ldots, z_{k-1}$ are roots of $U_k(z)$ as well. Thus all roots of the polynomial $U_k(z)$ of degree $k - 1$ are known and therefore $U_k(1) = 1 - mp/k$ determines $U_k(z)$, and consequently $U(z)$, uniquely. Since the series of $U(z)$ is absolutely convergent at $z = 1$, the system is ergodic and the expansion of $U(z)$ in powers of z furnishes the required probabilities P_j.

17. The Markov chain in question is irreducible and aperiodic, and since the system of equations (28) has a non-vanishing solution which forms an absolutely convergent series it is also ergodic. Equation (28) has now the following form

$$P_j = \sum_{i=0}^{\infty} P_i p_{ij}, \qquad (j = 0, 1, 2, \ldots).$$

Introducing the generating function

$$U(z) = \sum_{j=0}^{\infty} P_j z^j,$$

we obtain

$$U(z) = e^{\lambda(z-1)} U[1 + p(z - 1)].$$

Applying this formula repeatedly we obtain

$$U(z) = e^{\lambda(z-1)(1+p+\cdots+p^{n-1})} U[1 + p^n(z - 1)].$$

If $n \longrightarrow \infty$, then $p^n \longrightarrow 0$, and since $U(1) = 1$ we have finally

$$U(z) = e^{\lambda(z-1)/q},$$

and thus

$$P_j = e^{-\lambda/q} \frac{(\lambda/q)^j}{j!}, \qquad (j = 0, 1, 2, \ldots).$$

In this way we conclude that the system is ergodic and that the limiting distribution is a Poisson distribution.

18. This Markov chain is irreducible and periodic with period $t = 2$ and its states can be divided into two sub-sets,

$$G_0 = \{E_2, E_4, \ldots, E_{2a}\} \quad \text{and} \quad G_1 = \{E_1, E_3, \ldots, E_{2a-1}\}.$$

Now we have

$$p_{ij}^{(2)} = \begin{cases} p^2 & \text{if } j \equiv i + 2 \pmod{2a} \\ 2pq & \text{if } j \equiv i \pmod{2a} \\ q^2 & \text{if } j \equiv i - 2 \pmod{2a} \end{cases}$$

and

$$\lim_{n \to \infty} p_{ij}^{(2n)} = \begin{cases} P & \text{if } E_i \text{ and } E_j \text{ belong to the same set,} \\ 0 & \text{otherwise,} \end{cases}$$

$$\lim_{n \to \infty} p_{ij}^{(2n+1)} = \begin{cases} P_j & \text{if } E_i \text{ and } E_j \text{ belong to different sets,} \\ 0 & \text{otherwise.} \end{cases}$$

Now $\sum_{G_0} P_j = 1$ and $\sum_{G_1} P_j = 1$ and the quantities P_j satisfy the following system of equations

$$P_j = p^2 P_{j-2} + 2pq P_j + q^2 P_{j+2} \quad (j = 1, 2, \ldots, 2a),$$

where $P_{2a+1} = P_1$ and $P_0 = P_{2a}$. Whence we find $P_j = 1/a$ for all j. The stationary distribution is $P_j^* = 1/2a \quad (j = 1, 2, \ldots, 2a)$, which can be obtained according to (24) by solving the following system of equations:

$$P_j^* = p P_{j-1}^* + q P_{j+1}^* \quad (j = 1, 2, \ldots, 2a)$$

where $P_{2a+1}^* = P_1^*$ and $P_0^* = P_{2a}^*$. Clearly we have $P_j^* = \frac{1}{2} P_j$.

19. The transition probabilities p_{jk} can be easily obtained. We have

$$p_{jk} = \sum_{k_1 + k_2 + \ldots + k_j = k} p_{k_1} p_{k_2} \ldots p_{k_j}.$$

If we introduce the generating function

$$u(z) = \sum_{j=0}^{\infty} p_j z^j,$$

then p_{jk} will be the coefficient of z^k in the expansion of $[u(z)]^j$.

In the Markov chain in question the only absorbing state is E_0 (the number of elements of the assembly is zero) while the other states are transient. According to (22) the absorption probabilities π_j^* can be determined by solving the following system of equations

$$\pi_j^* = \sum_{\nu=1}^{\infty} p_{j\nu}\pi_\nu^* + p_{j0}, \qquad (j = 1, 2, \ldots).$$

$\pi_j^* = \lambda^j$ is a solution of this system if λ is a root of $u(\lambda) = \lambda$. It may be shown that the required root of $u(\lambda) = \lambda$ is the one with the smallest absolute value. If

$$u'(1) = \sum_{j=0}^{\infty} jp_j \leqq 1$$

but $p_1 \neq 1$ then $\lambda = 1$. If $u'(1) > 1$, then $\lambda < 1$ and if $p_0 = 0$, then $\lambda = 0$.

20. In the Markov chain in question E_1 is transient state and $\{E_2, E_3, E_4, E_5\}$ forms a closed set of states. The period of this closed set is $t = 4$. The eigenvalues of the transition probability matrix π are $\lambda_1 = \frac{1}{2}$, $\lambda_2 = 1$, $\lambda_3 = -1$, $\lambda_4 = i$, $\lambda_5 = -i$. Let x_j denote one of the left column vectors and y_j' one of the right row vectors belonging to the eigenvalue λ_j, and let them be chosen in such a way that $y_j'x_j = $ constant $(j = 1, 2, 3, 4, 5)$. Forming the following matrices:

$$\mathbf{A} = \| \mathbf{x}_1, \mathbf{x}_2, \mathbf{x}_3, \mathbf{x}_4, \mathbf{x}_5 \| \quad \text{and} \quad \mathbf{B} = \left\| \begin{matrix} \mathbf{y}_1' \\ \mathbf{y}_2' \\ \mathbf{y}_3' \\ \mathbf{y}_4' \\ \mathbf{y}_5' \end{matrix} \right\|.$$

we have explicitly

$$\mathbf{A} = \left\| \begin{matrix} \frac{2}{3} & 1 & \frac{1}{3} & 0 & 0 \\ 0 & 1 & -1 & i & -i \\ 0 & 1 & 1 & -1 & -1 \\ 0 & 1 & -1 & -i & i \\ 0 & 1 & 1 & 1 & 1 \end{matrix} \right\| \quad \text{and} \quad \mathbf{B} = \left\| \begin{matrix} 6 & -1 & -2 & -1 & -2 \\ 0 & 1 & 1 & 1 & 1 \\ 0 & -1 & 1 & -1 & 1 \\ 0 & -i & -1 & i & 1 \\ 0 & i & -1 & -i & 1 \end{matrix} \right\|$$

Now $AB = 4I$ and $\pi = \frac{1}{4}A\Lambda B$ where Λ is a diagonal matrix with elements λ_1, λ_2, λ_3, λ_4, λ_5. According to the equation (10) we can write

$$p_{13}^{(n)} = \frac{1}{4} + \frac{(-1)^n}{12} - \frac{1}{3}\left(\frac{1}{2}\right)^n.$$

If $\qquad n \equiv 0 \pmod{2}$, $\qquad$ then $\lim_{n \to \infty} p_{13}^{(n)} = \frac{1}{3}$;

if $\qquad n \equiv 1 \pmod{2}$, $\qquad$ then $\lim_{n \to \infty} p_{13}^{(n)} = \frac{1}{6}$.

21. In this case we can write $\xi_n = (\xi_{n-1} + \chi_{n-1})e^{-\alpha(\tau_n - \tau_{n-1})}$ and thus the transition probabilities are

$$\mathbf{P}\{\xi_n \leq x \mid \xi_{n-1} = y\} = \int_0^\infty H(xe^{\alpha u} - y)\, dG(u) = K(x, y).$$

If $\mathbf{E}\{\chi_n\} = \mu$ (the expectation of χ_n) is finite and $G(0) < 1$, then the Markov chain $\{\xi_n\}$ is ergodic and $P(x)$ is the unique solution of the following integral equation:

$$P(x) = \int_0^\infty K(x, y)\, dP(y).$$

This is proved as follows. Let us suppose first as a special case $\xi_0 \equiv 0$. We shall show that the sequence of distribution functions $\mathbf{P}\{\xi_n \leq x\} = P_n(x)$ $(n = 0, 1, 2, \ldots)$ is monotone non-increasing for a fixed x. We can write

$$\xi_n = \chi_0 e^{-\alpha(\tau_n - \tau_0)} + \chi_1 e^{-\alpha(\tau_n - \tau_1)} + \ldots + \chi_{n-1} e^{-\alpha(\tau_n - \tau_{n-1})}$$

and $\xi_{n+1} = \chi_0 e^{-\alpha(\tau_{n+1} - \tau_0)} + \xi_n^*$ where ξ_n and ξ_n^* are identically distributed random variables. Since $\chi_0 e^{-\alpha(\tau_{n+1} - \tau_0)} \geq 0$ we find

$$P_{n+1}(x) \leq P_n(x).$$

Furthermore, $0 \leq P_n(x) \leq 1$. Therefore there exists a limiting function $\lim_{n \to \infty} P_n(x) = P(x)$, which is obviously a non-decreasing function of x. We have to show that $P(x)$ is a distribution function. $P(0) = 0$ and therefore only $P(\infty) = 1$ is to be proved. Let

$$\beta = \int_0^\infty e^{-\alpha x}\, dG(x)$$

and $M_n = \mathbf{E}\{\xi_n\}$, then we have $M_{n+1} = (M_n + \mu)\beta$. Now $M_0 = 0$ and the sequence $\{M_n\}$ is monotone increasing and approaches $M = \mu\beta/(1 - \beta)$. Let $\varepsilon > 0$ and $x > M/\varepsilon$, then $x > M_n/\varepsilon$ holds also, and according to the well-known Markov inequality‡ for non-negative random variables we have for all arbitrarily small $\varepsilon > 0$ and for all n that $P_n(x) \geq 1 - \varepsilon$. Consequently $P(x) \geq 1 - \varepsilon$ if $x > M/\varepsilon$, which proves that $P(\infty) = 1$. Up to now we have had $\xi_0 \equiv 0$. However, if ξ_0 is arbitrary, then there is also a limiting distribution $P(x)$ which is the same as before. Namely, for an arbitrary ξ_0, ξ_n will differ from its former value only in one term $\xi_0 e^{-\alpha(\tau_n - \tau_0)}$ and this term converges stochastically to 0 when $n \to \infty$. Thus we conclude that the limiting distribution $P(x)$ is independent of the initial distribution of ξ_0 and the Markov chain $\{\xi_n\}$ is ergodic. If there is a limiting distribution, then it obviously satisfies the integral equation (32). We shall show that $P(x)$ is the unique solution of the integral equation in question. Suppose that there is another solution which is a distribution function, then this would be a stationary distribution. If we choose this distribution as the distribution of ξ_0, then the distribution of every ξ_n ($n = 0, 1, 2, \ldots$), and therefore also the limiting distribution, will be identical with it. However, we have already seen that $P(x)$ is the only limiting distribution and thus our assumption has led to a contradiction.

If in particular $\chi_n \equiv \mu$ is a constant, then

$$P(x) = \int_{x-\mu}^{\infty} \left[1 - G\left(\frac{1}{\alpha} \log \frac{\mu + y}{x}\right) \right] dP(y)$$

is the integral equation to be solved.

In case (a) this gives

$$P(x) = x^{\lambda/\alpha} \left[A - \frac{\lambda}{\alpha} \int_0^{x-\mu} \frac{P(y)}{(y + \mu)^{(1+\lambda/\alpha)}} \, dy \right],$$

where A is a constant. Using this recursive formula $P(x)$ can successively be calculated in each of the following intervals $(0, \mu)$, $(\mu, 2\mu)$, ... The constant A is determined by the requirement that

‡ Let $\xi \geq 0$ be a random variable, whose expectation $\mathbf{E}\{\xi\} = a$ exists, then it holds for arbitrary $\varepsilon > 0$ that $\mathbf{P}\left\{\xi > \dfrac{a}{\varepsilon}\right\} < \varepsilon$.

$P(\infty) = 1$. Thus we obtain

$$A = \frac{1}{\Gamma\left(1 + \dfrac{\lambda}{\alpha}\right)(\mu\gamma)^{\lambda/\alpha}},$$

where $\gamma = e^C = 1{\cdot}781072\ldots$ ($C = 0{\cdot}577215\ldots$ is Euler's constant.)

In case (b) $P(x)$ can be determined successively in each of the intervals $(\mu e^{-\alpha\tau} + \ldots + \mu e^{-k\alpha\tau}, \mu e^{-\alpha\tau} + \ldots + \mu e^{-(k+1)\alpha\tau})$, $(k = 1, 2, \ldots)$ by the recurrence formula

$$P(x) = e^{\lambda\tau}x^{\lambda/\alpha}\left[A - \frac{\lambda}{\alpha}\int_\mu^{xe^{\alpha\tau}} \frac{P(y - \mu)}{y^{(1+\lambda/\alpha)}}\,dy\right].$$

$P(x) = 1$ if $x \geq \mu/(e^{\alpha\tau} - 1)$. The value of A is the same as that of (a).

22. The Markovian character can easily be proved from the joint distribution of $(\xi_1, \xi_2, \ldots, \xi_m)$. The transition probabilities have the following form:

$$\mathbf{P}\{\xi_n \leq x \mid \xi_{n-1} = y\} = \begin{cases} 1 - \left(\dfrac{x - y}{1 - y}\right)^{m-n} & \text{if } 0 \leq y \leq x \leq 1, \\[2mm] 0 & \text{otherwise.} \end{cases}$$

23. Now we can write $\xi_n = [\xi_{n-1} + \chi_{n-1} - (\tau_n - \tau_{n-1})]^+$. ($[a]^+ = a$ if $a \geq 0$ and $[a]^+ = 0$ if $a \leq 0$.) The transition probabilities are

$$\mathbf{P}\{\xi_n \leq x \mid \xi_{n-1} = y\} = \int_0^\infty [1 - F(u + y - x)]\,dH(u) = K(x, y).$$

Consider first the special case when $\xi_0 \equiv 0$. Let
$$\vartheta_n = \chi_{n-1} - (\tau_n - \tau_{n-1}).$$

We have $\mathbf{P}\{\xi_n \leq x\} = 0$ if $x < 0$ and

$$\mathbf{P}\{\xi_n \leq x\} = \mathbf{P}\{\vartheta_1 + \vartheta_2 + \ldots + \vartheta_n \leq x, \vartheta_2 + \vartheta_3 + \ldots \\ + \vartheta_n \leq x, \ldots, \vartheta_n \leq x\},$$

if $x \geq 0$, which can be proved by induction. Since the random variables $\{\vartheta_n\}$ are independent and identically distributed we can write also that

$$\mathbf{P}\{\xi_n \leq x\} = \mathbf{P}\{\vartheta_1 \leq x, \vartheta_1 + \vartheta_2 \leq x, \ldots, \\ \vartheta_1 + \vartheta_2 + \ldots + \vartheta_n \leq x\}$$

for $x \geq 0$, or by introducing the notation $\Delta_r = \vartheta_1 + \vartheta_2 + \ldots + \vartheta_r$, $(r = 1, 2, \ldots)$ we have

$$\mathbf{P}\{\xi_n \leq x\} = \mathbf{P}\{\max_{1 \leq r \leq n} \Delta_r \leq x\}.$$

This shows that $P_n(x) = \mathbf{P}\{\xi_n \leq x\}$ $(n = 0, 1, 2, \ldots)$ forms a monotone decreasing sequence for a fixed x and therefore it converges to a limit $\lim_{n \to \infty} P_n(x) = P(x)$. This $P(x)$ is non-negative, non-decreasing and $P(x) = 0$ if $x < 0$. The question is, when will $P(x)$ be a distribution function, that is, when will $P(\infty) = 1$? We shall distinguish three cases corresponding to different mean values of ϑ_n.

If $\mathbf{E}\{\vartheta_n\} > 0$, then the strong law of large numbers shows that $P(x) \equiv 0$ for all x.

If $\mathbf{E}\{\vartheta_n\} < 0$, then it follows also from the strong law of large numbers that $P(\infty) = 1$; that is, $P(x)$ is a distribution function.

If $\mathbf{E}\{\vartheta_n\} = 0$ but $\vartheta_n \not\equiv 0$, then $P(x) \equiv 0$.

Thus if $\mathbf{E}\{\vartheta_n\} < 0$, there exists a limiting distribution $P(x)$ which satisfies the integral equation (32). It can be shown easily that the limiting distribution $P(x)$ is independent of the initial distribution of ξ_0. $P(x)$ is the unique solution of (32) since in this case there is only one stationary distribution.

24. Now according to (34)

$$f(\lambda) = \frac{1}{2\pi} \sum_{n=-\infty}^{\infty} R(n)e^{-in\lambda} = \frac{1}{2\pi} \frac{1-a^2}{|e^{i\lambda} - a|^2}, \qquad (-\pi \leq \lambda \leq \pi),$$

therefore $f(\lambda) \geq 0$, and $f(\lambda)$ is a density function which shows that $R(n)$ is a correlation function.

25. If $n \geq 0$, then

$$\mathbf{E}\{\xi_0 \xi_n\} = (1 - a^2) \sum_{k=n}^{\infty} a^k a^{k-n} = a^n,$$

and since $R(-n) = R(n)$ we have $R(n) = a^{|n|}$ for all n.

26. By substituting $z = e^{i\lambda}$ we obtain

$$R(n) = \int_{-\pi}^{\pi} e^{in\lambda} f(\lambda) \, d\lambda = \frac{C}{2\pi i} \oint_{|z|=1} \frac{z^{n-1}(z-b)\left(\dfrac{1}{z} - b\right)}{(z-a)\left(\dfrac{1}{z} - a\right)} \, dz$$

$$= \frac{C}{2\pi i} \oint_{|z|=1} z^{n-1} \left[\frac{b}{a} + \frac{(a-b)(1-ab)}{a(1-a^2)} \left(\frac{a}{z-a} + \frac{1}{1-az} \right) \right] dz$$

and according to the theorem of residues

$$R(n) = \begin{cases} C \dfrac{(1-2ab-b^2)}{1-a^2} & \text{if } n = 0 \\[2mm] C \dfrac{(a-b)(1-ab)a^{|n|-1}}{1-a^2} & \text{if } n \neq 0. \end{cases}$$

The constant C is determined by the requirement that $R(0) = 1$.

27. Let

$$\Phi_m^*(z) = \sum_{k=1}^{\infty} a_k z^{-k}.$$

In our problem

$$f^*(z) = \frac{C}{2\pi} \frac{(z-b)(1-bz)}{(z-a)(1-az)}.$$

Since

$$\frac{C}{2\pi} \frac{[z^m - \Phi_m^*(z)](z-b)(1-bz)}{(z-a)(1-az)}$$

is regular in $|z| \leq 1$, therefore $\Phi_m^*(a) = a^m$ and $\Phi_m^*(z)$ can have at most one pole of order one at $z = b$ in the unit circle $|z| \leq 1$. Thus we have $\Phi_m^*(z) = \gamma_m(z)/(z-b)$, where $\gamma_m(z)$ is an entire function such that $\gamma_m(a) = a^m(a-b)$. Finally $\Phi_m^*(\infty) = 0$ implies that $\gamma_m(z)$ is constant, so that

$$\Phi_m^*(z) = \frac{a^m(a-b)}{(z-b)}$$

and

$$\Phi_m(\lambda) = \frac{(a-b)a^m}{e^{i\lambda} - b} = (a-b)a^m \sum_{k=1}^{\infty} b^{k-1} e^{-ik\lambda}.$$

Accordingly

$$\xi_{n+m} \sim a^m(a-b)(\xi_{n-1} + b\xi_{n-2} + b^2\xi_{n-3} + \ldots)$$

and

$$\sigma_m^2 = C \left[1 + \frac{(a-b)^2(1-a^{2m})}{1-a^2} \right],$$

where

$$C = \frac{1 - a^2}{1 - 2ab - b^2}.$$

2. Markov processes

1. The expectation of the random variable ξ_t is $\mathbf{E}\{\xi_t\} = \lambda t$. This means that λ is the average number of atoms which decay during a unit length of time. (The variance of ξ_t is $\mathbf{D}^2\{\xi_t\} = \lambda t$.) The strong law of large numbers shows that

$$\mathbf{P}\left\{\lim_{t \to \infty} \frac{\xi_t}{t} = \lambda\right\} = 1.$$

This is true since $\{\xi_t\}$ is an additive Markov process, therefore ξ_t can be represented as the sum of identically distributed independent random variables. Consequently, if $t \to \infty$, then ξ_t/t will converge with probability 1 to λ; that is, λ can be interpreted as the temporal density of the occurrence of events. The probability that in the Poisson process there occurs exactly one event during $(t, t + \Delta t)$ is $\mathbf{P}\{\xi_{t+\Delta t} - \xi_t = 1\} = e^{-\lambda \Delta t}\lambda \Delta t = \lambda \Delta t + o(\Delta t)$ and the probability that there occurs more than one event is: $\mathbf{P}\{\xi_{t+\Delta t} - \xi_t > 1\} = 1 - e^{-\lambda \Delta t}(1 + \lambda \Delta t) = o(\Delta t)$. Thus λ is the probability density of the occurrence of the events.

2. As the process $\{\xi_t\}$ is additive, the time differences $\tau_{n+1} - \tau_n$ $(n = 1, 2, \ldots)$ are independent random variables. Now it holds independently of y, that

$$\mathbf{P}\{\tau_{n+1} - \tau_n \leq x \mid \tau_n = y\} = \mathbf{P}\{\xi_{y+x} - \xi_y > 0\}$$
$$= 1 - P_0(x) = 1 - e^{-\lambda x}$$

if $x \geq 0$. Consequently we have unconditionally that

$$\mathbf{P}\{\tau_{n+1} - \tau_n \leq x\} = 1 - e^{-\lambda x}$$

for $x \geq 0$. The case when $x < 0$ is obvious. (Hence it follows that $\mathbf{E}\{\tau_{n+1} - \tau_n\} = 1/\lambda$, which yields a new interpretation of the parameter λ : λ is equal to the reciprocal value of the expected length of time between two consecutive occurrences.)

3. $\mathbf{P}\{\eta_t \leq x\} = \mathbf{P}\{\xi_{t+x} - \xi_t > 0\}$ holds since $\eta_t \leq x$ if and only if there occurs at least one event during the time interval $(t, t + x)$. Now $\mathbf{P}\{\xi_{t+x} - \xi_t > 0\} = 1 - P_0(x) = 1 - e^{-\lambda x}$ for $x \geq 0$.

4. The process $\{\zeta_t\}$ is obviously a homogeneous, additive Markov process. By the theorem of total probability we have

$$\mathbf{P}\{\zeta_{t+u} - \zeta_u = k\} = \sum_{n=k}^{\infty} \mathbf{P}\{\xi_{t+u} - \xi_u = n\}\binom{n}{k}p^k(1-p)^{n-k},$$

that is,

$$\mathbf{P}\{\zeta_{t+u} - \zeta_u = k\}$$

$$= \sum_{n=k}^{\infty} e^{-\lambda t}\frac{(\lambda t)^n}{n!}\binom{n}{k}p^k(1-p)^{n-k} = e^{-\lambda pt}\frac{(\lambda pt)^k}{k!}.$$

Consequently $\{\zeta_t\}$ is a Poisson process.

5. The question is whether the approximation $N_k \sim Ne^{-a}a^k/k!$ holds good. Determine a from the requirement that the average number of observations during time t should coincide with the expected value calculated from the Poisson distribution, that is

$$a = \sum_{k=0}^{\infty} kN_k/N = 10{,}094/2{,}608 = 3{\cdot}870.$$

Using this value of a, we obtain

k	0	1	2	3	4	5
N_k	57	203	383	525	532	408
$\dfrac{Ne^{-a}a^k}{k!}$	54·399	210·523	407·361	525·496	508·418	393·515

k	6	7	8	9	≥ 10	total
N_k	273	139	45	27	16	2608
$\dfrac{Ne^{-a}a^k}{k!}$	253·817	140·325	67·882	29·189	17·075	2608

The agreement is satisfactory.

G

6. The process $\{\xi_t + \eta_t\}$ is obviously an additive Markov process. Let $\zeta = \xi_t + \eta_t$. Since

$$
\begin{aligned}
\mathbf{P}\{\zeta_{u+t} - \zeta_u = n\} &= \sum_{j=0}^{n} \mathbf{P}\{\xi_{u+t} - \xi_u = j\} \\
&\qquad \cdot \mathbf{P}\{\eta_{u+t} - \eta_u = n - j\} \\
&= \sum_{j=0}^{n} e^{-\lambda t} \frac{(\lambda t)^j}{j!} e^{-\mu t} \frac{(\mu t)^{n-j}}{(n-j)!} \\
&= e^{-(\lambda+\mu)t} \frac{[(\lambda + \mu)t]^n}{n!},
\end{aligned}
$$

therefore $\{\zeta_t\}$ is really a homogeneous Poisson process.

7. Let $0 \leq x_1 \leq x_2 \leq \ldots \leq x_n \leq t$. We can write

$$
\mathbf{P}\{\tau_1 \leq x_1, \tau_2 \leq x_2, \ldots, \tau_n \leq x_n \mid \xi_t = n\}
$$

$$
= \frac{\mathbf{P}\{\tau_1 \leq x_1, \tau_2 \leq x_2, \ldots, \tau_n \leq x_n, \xi_t = n\}}{\mathbf{P}\{\xi_t = n\}}
$$

$$
= \frac{1}{e^{-\lambda t} \dfrac{(\lambda t)^n}{n!}} \sum_{\{j_1, j_2, \ldots, j_n\}} e^{-\lambda x_1} \frac{(\lambda x_1)^{j_1}}{j_1!} e^{-\lambda(x_2 - x_1)} \frac{[\lambda(x_2 - x_1)]^{j_2}}{j_2!} \cdots
$$

$$
\cdot\, e^{-\lambda(x_n - x_{n-1})} \frac{[\lambda(x_n - x_{n-1})]^{j_n}}{j_n!} e^{-\lambda(t - x_n)}
$$

$$
= \sum_{\{j_1, j_2, \ldots, j_n\}} \frac{n!}{j_1! j_2! \ldots j_n!} \left(\frac{x_1}{t}\right)^{j_1} \left(\frac{x_2 - x_1}{t}\right)^{j_2} \ldots \left(\frac{x_n - x_{n-1}}{t}\right)^{j_n},
$$

where the summation is extended over all those sets of non-negative integers $\{j_1, j_2, \ldots, j_n\}$ for which $j_1 + j_2 + \ldots + j_n = n$ and $j_1 + j_2 + \ldots + j_k \geq k$ $(k = 1, 2, \ldots, n - 1)$. The identity of the two distributions in question can be seen immediately.

8. The event $\eta_t = k$ may occur in several mutually exclusive ways: in the Poisson process $n = 0, 1, \ldots$ events occur during time $(0, t]$. If the number of events is n, then from amongst the corresponding n electrons k must still be in the space and $n - k$ must already have disappeared at time t. The probability that an electron which leaves the cathode at an instant distributed uniformly in the interval $(0, t]$ will still be in the space at time t is

$$
p_t = \frac{1}{t} \int_0^t [1 - H(x)] \, dx.
$$

Using the solution of Problem 4 we can write, on account of the theorem of total probability,

$$\mathbf{P}\{\eta_t = k\} = \sum_{n=k}^{\infty} \mathbf{P}\{\xi_t = n\}\binom{n}{k}p_t^k[1 - p_t]^{n-k}$$

$$= e^{-\lambda \int_0^t [1 - H(x)]dx} \frac{\left[\lambda \int_0^t [1 - H(x)]\, dx\right]^k}{k!}$$

If the mean value of the distribution $F(x)$ exists, i.e.

$$\alpha = \int_0^\infty x\, dF(x) < \infty,$$

then it also holds that

$$\alpha = \int_0^\infty [1 - F(x)]\, dx$$

and consequently

$$\lim_{t \to \infty} \mathbf{P}\{\eta_t = k\} = e^{-\lambda\alpha} \frac{(\lambda\alpha)^k}{k!}.$$

9. The correlation coefficient is defined by

$$\mathbf{R}\{\xi_t, \xi_{t+\tau}\} = \frac{\mathbf{E}\{\xi_t\,\xi_{t+\tau}\} - \mathbf{E}\{\xi_t\}\mathbf{E}\{\xi_{t+\tau}\}}{\mathbf{D}\{\xi_t\}\mathbf{D}\{\xi_{t+\tau}\}}.$$

Now $\mathbf{E}\{\xi_t\} = \lambda t$, $\mathbf{D}\{\xi_t\} = \sqrt{\lambda t}$ and $\mathbf{E}\{\xi_t\xi_{t+\tau}\} = \mathbf{E}\{\xi_t^2\}$ $+ \mathbf{E}\{\xi_t(\xi_{t+\tau} - \xi_t)\} = \mathbf{E}\{\xi_t^2\} + \mathbf{E}\{\xi_t\}\mathbf{E}\{\xi_{t+\tau} - \xi_t\} = \lambda t(\lambda t + \lambda\tau + 1)$ because ξ_t and $\xi_{t+\tau} - \xi_t$ are independent. Thus finally

$$\mathbf{R}\{\xi_t, \xi_{t+\tau}\} = \sqrt{t/(t + \tau)}.$$

10. If we suppose that $\xi_0 = 0$ and introduce the notation

$$\mathbf{P}\{\xi_t = n\} = P_n(t),$$

then it holds in general that $\mathbf{P}\{\xi_t - \xi_s = n\} = P_n(t - s)$. It is obviously true that

$$(*) \qquad P_n(t + s) = \sum_{k=0}^{n} P_k(t)P_{n-k}(s), \qquad (n = 0, 1, 2, \ldots).$$

This system of functional equations successively determines the unknowns $P_0(t)$, $P_1(t)$, $P_2(t)$, ... It follows first from $P_0(t + s) = P_0(t)P_0(s)$ that $P_0(t) = e^{-\lambda t}$ for $\lambda \geq 0$ because the probability $_0(t)$ is a non-increasing function of t. Now by induction we justify that

$$P_n(t) = e^{-\lambda t} \sum \frac{(c_1 t)^{j_1} (c_2 t)^{j_2} \dots (c_n t)^{j_n}}{j_1! j_2! \dots j_n!},$$

where the summation is for $j_1 + 2j_2 + \dots nj_n = n$.

Assume the formula to be valid for $k = 0, 1, 2, \dots, n - 1$ and let

$$f(t) = e^{\lambda t} P_n(t) - \sum \frac{(c_1 t)^{j_1} (c_2 t)^{j_2} \dots (c_{n-1} t)^{j_{n-1}}}{j_1! j_2! \dots j_n!},$$

where the summation is for $j_1 + 2j_2 + \dots + (n - 1)j_{n-1} = n$; then, because of (*), it holds that $f(t + s) = f(t) + f(s)$. The only solution of this functional equation which is bounded in any one finite interval is $f(t) = c_n t$, which proves the statement for $k = n$.

It follows from the formula of $P_n(t)$ that

$$\lim_{t \to 0} \frac{P_n(t)}{t} = c_n$$

and therefore $c_n \geq 0$. Furthermore,

$$\sum_{n=0}^{\infty} P_n(t) = 1 \quad \text{implies that} \quad \lambda = \sum_{n=1}^{\infty} c_n.$$

Note that a compound Poisson process $\{\xi_t\}$ can be represented in the following form:

$$\xi_t = \sum_{n=1}^{\infty} n \, \xi_t^{(n)}$$

where $\{\xi_t^{(n)}\}$ are mutually independent Poisson processes, and $\xi_t^{(n)}$ has density c_n.

11. Decompose the set A into a sum of disjoint sets of identical measures as follows: $A = A_n^{(1)} + A_n^{(2)} + \dots + A_n^{(n)}$. Let A_n be an arbitrary set of this decomposition and let $\mathbf{E}\{e^{iz\xi(A)}\} = \phi_A(z)$; then we have for all n that $\phi_A(z) = [\phi_{A_n}(z)]^n$. Furthermore,

$$\mathbf{P}\{\xi(A) = 0\} = [\mathbf{P}\{\xi(A_n) = 0\}]^n.$$

Now on the one hand we can use condition 4° to write

$$\mathbf{P}\{\xi(A) = 0\} = e^{-\lim_{n \to \infty} n\mathbf{P}\{\xi(A_n)=1\}},$$

and on the other hand

$$\phi_A(z) = \exp\left[(1 - e^{iz})\lim_{n \to \infty} n\mathbf{P}\{\xi(A_n) = 1\}\right].$$

Therefore

$$\phi_A(z) = [\mathbf{P}\{\xi(A) = 0\}]^{(e^{iz}-1)},$$

which is the characteristic function of a Poisson distribution. Since $\mathbf{P}\{\xi(A) = 0\} = e^{-\mathbf{E}\{\xi(A)\}}$, therefore $\mathbf{E}\{\xi(A)\}$ is an additive set function of $\mu(A)$ and thus $\mathbf{E}\{\xi(A)\} = \lambda\mu(A)$ for some $\lambda > 0$.

12. Let δ_P denote the distance of a star at point P from its nearest neighbour. $\mathbf{P}\{\delta_P \leq r\} = 1 - \mathbf{P}\{\delta_P > r\} = 1 - e^{-\frac{4}{3}\pi r^3 \lambda}$, because $\delta_P > r$ if and only if there is no star in the sphere of radius r around P. Thus

$$\mathbf{E}\{\delta_P\} = 4\pi\lambda \int_0^\infty r^3 e^{-\frac{4}{3}\pi r^3 \lambda} dr$$

$$= \left(\frac{3}{4\lambda\pi}\right)^{1/3} \int_0^\infty x^{1/3} e^{-x} dx = \frac{3^{1/3}\Gamma\left(1 + \frac{1}{3}\right)}{(4\pi)^{1/3}\lambda^{1/3}} = \frac{0\cdot616\dots}{\lambda^{1/3}}.$$

13. If $\xi_t = n$, then it follows, by Problem 7, that the n points are distributed independently and uniformly on the circumference of the circle. Let the distances of neighbouring points be denoted by the random variables $\delta_1, \delta_2, \dots, \delta_n$. Let A_i be the event that $\delta_i > \alpha$. If there occur exactly k amongst the events $A_1, A_2, \dots, A_n$, then k points will not be covered amongst n. The probability of this event, $P_k\{A_1, A_2, \dots, A_n\}$ is furnished by a general probability theorem of *Ch. Jordan*.[†] In this case $A_1, A_2, \dots, A_n$ are equivalent events and we have

$$\mathbf{P}\{A_1 A_2 \dots A_j\} = \begin{cases} \left(1 - \dfrac{j\alpha}{t}\right)^{n-1} & \text{if } 0 \leq j\alpha \leq t, \\ \\ 0 & \text{otherwise.} \end{cases}$$

[†] Cf. L. Takács, 'On a general probability theorem and its applications in the theory of the stochastic processes', *Proc. Cambridge Phil. Soc.*, **54** (1958), 219–24.

Thus according to the general probability theorem we have

$$P_k\{A_1, A_2, \ldots, A_n\} = \binom{n}{k} \sum_{j=k}^{[t/\alpha]} (-1)^{j-k} \binom{n-k}{n-j} \left(1 - \frac{j\alpha}{t}\right)^{n-1},$$

and finally it follows by the theorem of total probability that

$$\mathbf{P}\{\eta_t = k\} = \sum_{n=k}^{\infty} e^{-\lambda t} \frac{(\lambda t)^n}{n!} \binom{n}{k} \sum_{j=k}^{[t/\alpha]} (-1)^{j-k} \binom{n-k}{n-j} \left(1 - \frac{j\alpha}{t}\right)^{n-1}$$

$$= \sum_{j=k}^{[t/\alpha]} (-1)^{j-k} \binom{j}{k} \frac{e^{-\lambda \alpha j} (\lambda t)^j}{j!} \left(1 - \frac{j\alpha}{t}\right)^{j-1}.$$

14. We have $\tau_n \leq t$ if and only if at least n events occur during $(0, t]$; that is,

$$\mathbf{P}\{\tau_n \leq t\} = \mathbf{P}\{\xi_t \geq n\} = 1 - \mathbf{P}\{\xi_t < n\} = 1 - \sum_{j=0}^{n-1} e^{-\lambda t} \frac{(\lambda t)^j}{j!}.$$

Therefore

$$G_n(t) = \begin{cases} 0 & \text{if } t < 0, \\ 1 - \sum_{j=0}^{n-1} e^{-\lambda t} \frac{(\lambda t)^j}{j!} & \text{if } t \geq 0. \end{cases}$$

The density function is $g_n(t) = G'_n(t)$; however, $g_n(t)$ can be directly obtained from the relation

$$\mathbf{P}\{t < \tau_n \leq t + \Delta t\} = g_n(t)\Delta t + o(\Delta t).$$

We have

$$\mathbf{P}\{t < \tau_n \leq t + \Delta t\} = \mathbf{P}\{\xi_t = n - 1\}$$
$$\cdot \mathbf{P}\{\xi_{t+\Delta t} - \xi_t > 0\} + o(\Delta t)$$
$$= e^{-\lambda t} \frac{(\lambda t)^{n-1}}{(n-1)!} \lambda \Delta t + o\Delta(t)$$

and thus

$$g_n(t) = \begin{cases} 0 & \text{if } t < 0, \\ e^{-\lambda t} \frac{(\lambda t)^{n-1}}{(n-1)!} \lambda & \text{if } t \geq 0. \end{cases}$$

Furthermore

$$\mathbf{E}\{\tau_n^s\} = \int_0^\infty t^s g_n(t) \, dt = \frac{\Gamma(n+s)}{\Gamma(n)\lambda^s}.$$

If s is a positive integer, then

$$\mathbf{E}\{\tau_n^s\} = \frac{n(n+1)\dots(n+s-1)}{\lambda^s}.$$

15. It is obvious that $\{\xi_t\}$ is a homogeneous, additive Markov process, and according to (15)

$$\frac{dP_{ik}(t)}{dt} = -\lambda P_{ik}(t) + \lambda P_{i,\,k-1}(t)$$

and the initial condition is

$$P_{ik}(0) = \begin{cases} 1 & \text{if } i = k, \\ 0 & \text{if } i \ne k. \end{cases}$$

The solution of this system of differential equations is

$$P_{ik}(t) = e^{-\lambda t} \frac{(\lambda t)^{k-i}}{(k-i)!} \quad \text{if } k \ge i.$$

Therefore $\{\xi_t\}$ is really a Poisson process.

16. In this case $\{\xi_t\}$ is a Markov process. Assume that at time t the system is in state E_n. Then the probability of a transition $E_n \longrightarrow E_{n+1}$ during $(t, t + \Delta t)$ is $\lambda \Delta t(1 - n\mu\Delta t) + o(\Delta t)$. For this event occurs if during $(t, t + \Delta t)$ a new call arrives at the centre (the probability of that is $\lambda \Delta t + o\Delta(t)$) and none of n conversations in progress terminate (the probability of which is $[1 - H(\Delta t)]^n = 1 - n\mu\Delta t + o(\Delta t)$). The probability of the transition $E_n \longrightarrow E_{n-1}$ during $(t, t + \Delta t)$ is $(1 - \lambda \Delta t)n\mu\Delta t + o(\Delta t)$. For this event occurs if there is no call arriving during $(t, t + \Delta t)$ (the probability of this event is $1 - \lambda \Delta t + o(\Delta t)$) and one of the conversations in progress terminates in the time interval $(t, t + \Delta t)$ (the probability of this event is $\binom{n}{1} H(\Delta t)[1 - H(\Delta t)]^{n-1} = n\mu\Delta t + o(\Delta t)$). The other transitions during $(t, t + \Delta t)$ have probability $o(\Delta t)$. The probability of no change during $(t, t + \Delta t)$ is $1 - (\lambda + n\mu)\Delta t + o(\Delta t)$, because $1 - \lambda \Delta t + o(\Delta t)$ is the probability that there is no call during $(t, t + \Delta t)$ and $[1 - H(\Delta t)]^n = 1 - n\mu\Delta t + o(\Delta t)$ is the probability that no conversation terminates during $(t, t + \Delta t)$. Accordingly, the process $\{\xi_t\}$ is homogeneous,

$$c_n = \lambda + n\mu, \qquad p_{n,n+1} = \frac{\lambda}{\lambda + n\mu}, \qquad p_{n,n-1} = \frac{n\mu}{\lambda + n\mu}$$

if $n = 0, 1, \ldots, m - 1$ and

$$c_m = m\mu, \qquad p_{m,m-1} = 1.$$

Now according to (21) we have

$$(\lambda + n\mu)P_n = \lambda P_{n-1} + (n + 1)\mu P_{n+1}, \quad (n = 0, 1, \ldots, m - 1),$$

where $P_{-1} = 0$, while for $n = m$ we have $m\mu P_m = \lambda P_{m-1}$. By this system of equations we obtain $n\mu P_n - \lambda P_{n-1} = (n + 1)\mu P_{n+1} - \lambda P_n$, $(n = 0, 1, \ldots, m - 1)$, that is, $n\mu P_n - \lambda P_{n-1} \equiv C$, constant independent of n. This constant C is equal to zero because it is equal to zero for $n = 0$ (and for $n \doteq m$). Thus

$$P_n = \frac{\lambda}{n\mu} P_{n-1},$$

and by repeated applications of this we obtain

$$P_n = \left(\frac{\lambda}{\mu}\right)^n \frac{1}{n!} P_0 \qquad (n = 0, 1, \ldots, m).$$

Since

$$\sum_{j=0}^{m} P_j = 1,$$

therefore

$$P_0 = 1 \bigg/ \sum_{j=0}^{m} \left(\frac{\lambda}{\mu}\right)^j \frac{1}{j!}$$

and finally

$$P_n = \frac{\dfrac{(\lambda/\mu)^n}{n!}}{\displaystyle\sum_{j=0}^{m} \dfrac{(\lambda/\mu)^j}{j!}} = \frac{e^{-\lambda/\mu} \dfrac{(\lambda/\mu)^n}{n!}}{\displaystyle\sum_{j=0}^{m} e^{-\lambda/\mu} \dfrac{(\lambda/\mu)^j}{j!}}.$$

Remark: Here we have made use of the fact that the probability that a conversation in progress at t will terminate during $(t, t + \Delta t)$

is $H(\Delta t)$ and this probability is independent of the past duration of the conversation. This is the well-known property of the exponential distribution

$$H(x) = 1 - e^{-\mu x} \quad (\text{if } x \geq 0).$$

For denote by τ the length of a conversation. The probability that the conversation terminates during $(u, u + x)$, given that it did not terminate in the time interval $(0, u]$ is

$$\mathbf{P}\{\tau \leq u + x \mid \tau \geq u\} = \frac{\mathbf{P}\{u < \tau \leq u + x\}}{\mathbf{P}\{u \leq \tau\}}$$

$$= \frac{H(u + x) - H(u)}{1 - H(u)} = H(x),$$

which is equal to $H(x)$ and is independent of u.

17. In this case $\{\xi_t\}$ is a homogeneous Markov process. If the system is in state E_j at time t, then the probability of no change during $(t, t + \Delta t)$ is $1 - j\lambda\Delta t - \mu\Delta t + o(\Delta t)$, the probability of the transition $E_j \longrightarrow E_{j+1}$ is $\mu\Delta t + o(\Delta t)$ and that of $E_j \longrightarrow E_{j-1}$ is $j\lambda\Delta t + o(\Delta t)$. The other transitions have probability $o(\Delta t)$. Now

$$c_j = \mu + j\lambda, \; p_{j,j+1} = \frac{\mu}{\mu + j\lambda}, \; p_{j,j-1} = \frac{j\lambda}{\mu + j\lambda},$$

if $j = 0, 1, \ldots, m-1$, and $c_m = m\lambda$, $p_{m,m-1} = 1$. We have by (21) that

$$(\mu + j\lambda)P = \mu P_{j-1} + (j + 1)\lambda P_{j+1}, \qquad (j = 0, 1, \ldots, m - 1),$$

where $P_{-1} = 0$ and $m\lambda P_m = \mu P_{m-1}$ for $j = m$. The equations above show that

$$j\lambda P_j - \mu P_{j-1} = (j + 1)\lambda P_{j+1} - \mu P_j, \qquad (j = 0, 1, \ldots, m - 1),$$

whose solution, similarly to that of Problem 16, is

$$P_j = \frac{(\mu/\lambda)^j}{j!} \Big/ \sum_{j=0}^{m} \frac{(\mu/\lambda)^j}{j!}.$$

The expected number of machines working simultaneously is

$$\sum_{j=1}^{m} jP_j = \frac{\mu}{\lambda} \sum_{j=1}^{m} P_{j-1} = \frac{\mu}{\lambda} (1 - P_m).$$

18. Now as before, the process $\{\xi_t\}$ is a homogeneous Markov process. $E_j \longrightarrow E_{j+1}$ and $E_j \longrightarrow E_{j-1}$ $(j = 0, 1, \ldots, m)$ are the possible transitions. Now we have

$$c_j = j\lambda + s\mu, \, p_{j, j+1} = \frac{s\mu}{j\lambda + s\mu}, \, p_{j, j-1} = \frac{j\lambda}{j\lambda + s\mu}$$

if $j = 0, 1, \ldots, m - s$ and

$$c_j = j\lambda + (m-j)\mu, \, p_{j, j+1} = \frac{(m-j)\mu}{j\lambda + (m-j)\mu}, \, p_{j, j-1} = \frac{j\lambda}{j\lambda + (m-j)\mu}$$

if $j = m - s + 1, m - s + 2, \ldots, m$. According to equation (21) we have

$$(j\lambda + s\mu)P_j = s\mu P_{j-1} + (j+1)\lambda P_{j+1}, \quad (j = 0, 1, \ldots, m - s - 1),$$

and

$$(j\lambda + (m-j)\mu)P_j = (m - j + 1)\mu P_{j-1} + (j+1)\lambda P_{j+1},$$
$$(j = m - s + 1, \ldots, m),$$

where $P_{m+1} = P_{-1} = 0$. Hence

$$j\lambda P_j - s\mu P_{j-1} = (j+1)\lambda P_{j+1} - s\mu P_j, \quad (j = 0, 1, \ldots, m - s - 1),$$

and

$$j\lambda P_j - (m - j + 1)\mu P_{j-1} = (j+1)\lambda P_{j+1} - (m-j)\mu P_j,$$
$$(j = m - s + 1, \ldots, m).$$

Consequently

$$P_j = \left(\frac{s\mu}{\lambda}\right)^j \frac{1}{j!} P_0 \quad \text{if} \quad j = 0, 1, \ldots, m - s - 1,$$

and

$$P_j = \left(\frac{\mu}{\lambda}\right)^{j-m+s+1} \frac{(m - j + 1) \ldots s . s}{j(j-1) \ldots (m-s)} P_{m-s-1}$$

$$= \left(\frac{\mu}{\lambda}\right) \frac{s^{m-s} (m - j + 1) \ldots s}{j!} P_0,$$

if $j = m - s, \ldots, m$. P_0 is to be determined from

$$\sum_{j=0}^{m} P_j = 1.$$

19. Let $q(t)$ denote the probability that a radioactive atom does not decay during time t. Obviously $q(t) \leq q(s)$ if $t < s$, and $q(t + s) =$

$q(t)q(s)$ if $t \geq 0$ and $s \geq 0$. This implies that $q(t) = e^{-\lambda t}$, where $\lambda > 0$. (The physically uninteresting case of $\lambda = 0$ is excluded.) If at time t the system is in state E_j, then the probability of the transition $E_j \longrightarrow E_{j-1}$ during time $(t, t + \Delta t)$ is

$$\binom{j}{1}[q(\Delta t)]^{j-1}[1 - q(\Delta t)] = j\lambda\Delta t + o(\Delta t).$$

The other transitions have probability $o(\Delta t)$. The process $\{\xi_t\}$ is a homogeneous Markov process with $c_j = j\lambda$ and $p_{j, j-1} = 1$. $\mathbf{P}\{\xi_t = j\} = P_j(t)$ is the solution of the system of differential equations

$$\frac{dP_j(t)}{dt} = -j\lambda P_j(t) + (j + 1)\lambda P_{j+1}(t), \qquad (j = 0, 1, \ldots, N)$$

where $P_{N+1}(t) \equiv 0$. The initial conditions are

$$P_j(0) = \begin{cases} 1 & \text{if } j = N, \\ 0 & \text{if } j \neq N. \end{cases}$$

The solution is

$$P_j(t) = \binom{N}{j} e^{-\lambda t j}(1 - e^{-\lambda t})^{N-j}.$$

The probability of $t < \tau_j \leq t + \Delta t$ is $P_{j-1}(t)(j - 1)\lambda\Delta t + o(\Delta t)$. Therefore the density function of τ_j is $f_j(t) = P_{j-1}(t)(j - 1)\lambda$ if $t \geq 0$, while $f_j(t) = 0$ if $t < 0$. Finally,

$$\mathbf{E}\{\tau_j\} = \int_0^\infty t f_j(t)\, dt$$

$$= \frac{1}{\lambda N} + \frac{1}{\lambda(N - 1)} + \ldots + \frac{1}{\lambda(j + 1)} \sim \frac{1}{\lambda} \log \frac{N}{j}.$$

If $j \sim \frac{1}{2}N$, then we obtain the expected half-value period which is $\sim (\log 2)/\lambda$.

20. If $\xi_t \equiv j$ (mod. m) impulses occur during $(0, t]$, then the system is said to be in state E_j at time t. Let

$$\mathbf{P}\{\xi_t \equiv j \,(\text{mod. } m)\} = P(t).$$

If we suppose that the system is in state E_j, then $\lambda\Delta t + o(\Delta t)$ is the probability that a transition $E_j \longrightarrow E_{j+1}$ occurs during $(t, t + \Delta t)$. The probabilities $\lim_{t \to \infty} P(t) = P$ can be determined by solving the following system of equations:

$$\lambda P_j = \lambda P_{j-1} \quad (j = 1, 2, \ldots, m - 1).$$

The solution is $P_j = 1/m$ $(j = 0, 1, \ldots, m - 1)$. Now by the theorem of total probability, we obtain

$$\mathbf{P}\{\eta_{t+u} - \eta_t = n\} = \sum_{j=0}^{m-1} \mathbf{P}\{\xi_t \equiv j \,(\text{mod. } m)\}$$

$$\cdot \mathbf{P}\{nm - j \leq \xi_{t+u} - \xi_t \leq (n + 1)m - j - 1\}$$

and therefore

$$\lim_{t \to \infty} \mathbf{P}\{\eta_{t+u} - \eta_t = n\} = \frac{1}{m} \sum_{j=0}^{m-1} \sum_{k=nm-j}^{(n+1)m-j-1} e^{-\lambda u} \frac{(\lambda u)^k}{k!}.$$

21. The process $\{\xi_t\}$ is a homogeneous Markov process with

$$c_j = j\mu + (m - j)\lambda, \qquad p_{j, j+1} = \frac{(m - j)\lambda}{j\mu + (m - j)\lambda},$$

$$p_{,j-1} = \frac{j\mu}{j\mu + (m - j)\lambda}.$$

If $\mathbf{P}(t) = \| P_{ik}(t) \|$, $(i, k = 0, 1, \ldots, m)$, then we can write, according to equation (19),

$$\mathbf{P}(t) = e^{\mathbf{A}t},$$

where $\mathbf{A} = \| a_{ij} \|$ with $a_{i, i-1} = \mu i$, $a_{i, i} = -\lambda(m - i) - \mu i$, $a_{i, i+1} = \lambda(m - i)$ and $a_{ij} = 0$ if $|j - i| > 1$.

Let us find the canonical form of $\mathbf{A}$. To this end we consider the equation $\mathbf{y}'\mathbf{A} = \omega \mathbf{y}'$, where $\mathbf{y}' = \| \beta_0, \beta_1, \ldots, \beta_m \|$. Writing this equation in detail we have

$$\lambda(m - k - 1)\beta_{k-1} - (\lambda(m - k) + \mu k)\beta_k$$
$$+ (k + 1)\mu\beta_{k+1} = \omega\beta_k \quad (k = 0, 1, \ldots, m).$$

If we introduce the generating function

$$U(z) = \sum_{k=0}^{m} \beta_k z^k$$

then we have

$$(1 - z)(\lambda z + \mu)U'(z) = [\omega + \lambda m(1 - z)]U(z)$$

and consequently

$$U(z) = C(1 - z)^{-\frac{\omega}{\lambda + \mu}} (\lambda z + \mu)^{m + \frac{\omega}{\lambda + \mu}}.$$

Since $U(z)$ is a polynomial of degree m, we must have $\omega = -j(\lambda + \mu)$, $(j = 0, 1, \ldots, m)$. The numbers $\omega_j = -j(\lambda + \mu)$ are the eigenvalues of Λ. If $\mathbf{y}_j' = \| \beta_{j0}, \beta_{j1}, \ldots, \beta_{jm} \|$ is the eigenvector belonging to the eigenvalue ω_j, then

$$\sum_{k=0}^{m} \beta_{jk} z^k = C_j (1 - z)^j (\lambda z + \mu)^{m-j},$$

where C_j is an arbitrary constant. Determine now the matrix $\| \alpha_{ij} \|$ satisfying the relation $\| \alpha_{ij} \| \, \| \beta_{jk} \| = \| \delta_{ik} \|$. The quantities α_{ij} can be obtained in the following way. First of all we can write

$$\begin{aligned}
z^i = \sum_{k=0}^{m} \delta_{ik} z^k &= \sum_{k=0}^{m} z^k \sum_{j=0}^{m} \alpha_{ij} \beta_{jk} \\
&= \sum_{j=0}^{m} \alpha_{ij} \sum_{k=0}^{m} \beta_{jk} z^k \\
&= \sum_{j=0}^{m} \alpha_{ij} C_j (1 - z)^j (\lambda z + \mu)^{m-j} \\
&= (\lambda z + \mu)^m \sum_{j=0}^{m} \alpha_{ij} C_j \left(\frac{1 - z}{\lambda z + \mu} \right)^j.
\end{aligned}$$

If we write $\zeta = (1 - z)/(\lambda z + \mu)$, then

$$\sum_{j=0}^{m} \alpha_{ij} C_j \zeta^j = \frac{(1 - \mu\zeta)^i (1 + \lambda\zeta)^{m-i}}{(\lambda + \mu)^m}.$$

Let $C_j = \mu^j / \sqrt{\mu^m (\lambda + \mu)^m}$, then it can be seen that $\| \alpha_{ij} \|$ and $\| \beta_{jk} \|$ are identical and

$$\sum_{j=0}^{m} \alpha_{ij} z^j = \frac{(\mu - \mu z)^i (\mu + \lambda z)^{m-i}}{\sqrt{\mu^m (\lambda + \mu)^m}}.$$

Let $\mathbf{H} = \| \alpha_{ij} \| = \| \beta_{jk} \|$. Now we have $\mathbf{A} = \mathbf{H}\Lambda\mathbf{H}$ where $\Lambda = \| \omega_j \delta_{ij} \|$ and $\mathbf{P}(t) = \mathbf{H} \| e^{\omega_j t}\delta_{ij} \| \mathbf{H}$ or

$$P_{ik}(t) = \sum_{j=0}^{m} \alpha_{ij}\alpha_{jk}e^{-j(\lambda + \mu)t}.$$

The generating function of $P_{ik}(t)$ can easily be obtained:

$$\sum_{k=0}^{m} P_{ik}(t)z^k = \sum_{j=0}^{m} \alpha_{ij}e^{-j(\lambda+\mu)t} \frac{(\mu - \mu z)^j(\mu + \lambda z)^{m-j}}{\sqrt{\mu^m(\lambda + \mu)^m}}$$

$$= \frac{[\mu + \lambda z - \mu(1-z)e^{-(\lambda+\mu)t}]^i[\mu + \lambda z + \lambda(1-z)e^{-(\lambda+\mu)t}]^{m-i}}{(\lambda + \mu)^m}.$$

Taking the limit $t \longrightarrow \infty$ in the equation above we obtain

$$\sum_{k=0}^{m} P_k z^k = \left(\frac{\lambda z + \mu}{\lambda + \mu} \right)^m$$

and, consequently,

$$P_k = \binom{m}{k}\left(\frac{\lambda}{\lambda + \mu} \right)^k\left(\frac{\mu}{\lambda + \mu} \right)^{m-k}.$$

22. The process $\{\xi_t\}$ is a homogeneous Markov process with $c_j = \lambda + j\mu$, $p_{j,j+1} = \lambda/(\lambda + j\mu)$ and $p_{j,j-1} = j\mu/(\lambda + j\mu)$. Let $\mathbf{P}(t) = \| P_{ik}(t) \|$, $(i, k = 0, 1, 2, \ldots)$. If we suppose first that the number of available channels is finite N and take the limit $N \longrightarrow \infty$, then we obtain that $\mathbf{P}(t) = e^{\mathbf{A}t}$, where $\mathbf{A} = \| a_{ij} \|$ with $a_{i,i-1} = \mu i$, $a_{ii} = -(\lambda + \mu i)$, $a_{i,i+1} = \lambda$ and $a_{ij} = 0$ if $|j - i| > 1$. Further, the spectrum of $\mathbf{A}$ is the set $\omega_j = -j\mu$ $(j = 0, 1, 2, \ldots)$. Let $\mathbf{y}' = \| \beta_0, \beta_1, \ldots \|$ and consider the equation $\mathbf{y}'\mathbf{A} = \omega\mathbf{y}'$ which is equivalent to the system of linear equations

$$\lambda\beta_{k-1} - (\lambda + k\mu)\beta_k + (k + 1)\mu\beta_{k+1} = \omega\beta_k, \ (k = 0, 1, 2, \ldots).$$

If

$$U(z) = \sum_{k=0}^{\infty} \beta_k z^k,$$

then

$$U'(z)\mu(1 - z) = [\omega + \lambda(1 - z)]U(z)$$

and hence

$$U(z) = Ce^{\lambda z/\mu}(1 - z)^{-\omega/\mu}.$$

If $\mathbf{y}_j' = \| \beta_{j0}, \beta_{j1}, \dots \|$ is the eigenvector belonging to $\omega = \omega_j = -j\mu$ then we have

$$\sum_{k=0}^{\infty} \beta_{jk}z^k = C_j e^{\lambda z/\mu}(1 - z)^j.$$

Determine now the inverse matrix of $\| \beta_{jk} \|$, that is the matrix $\mathbf{H} = \| \alpha_{ij} \|$ for which $\| \alpha_{ij} \| \, \| \beta_{jk} \| = \| \delta_{ik} \|$. With this notation we can write the following relation:

$$z^i = \sum_{k=0}^{\infty} \delta_{ik}z^k = \sum_{k=0}^{\infty} z^k \sum_{j=0}^{\infty} \alpha_{ij}\beta_{jk}$$

$$= \sum_{j=0}^{\infty} \alpha_{ij} \sum_{k=0}^{\infty} \beta_{jk}z^k = e^{\lambda z/\mu} \sum_{j=0}^{\infty} \alpha_{ij}C_j(1 - z)^j.$$

Let now $C_j = e^{-\lambda/2\mu}$, then we obtain

$$\sum_{j=0}^{\infty} \alpha_{ij}z^j = e^{-\frac{\lambda}{2\mu}(1-2z)}(1 - z)^i,$$

and furthermore $\| \alpha_{ij} \| = \| \beta_{jk} \|$.

Accordingly, $\mathbf{A} = \mathbf{H}\Lambda\mathbf{H}$, where $\Lambda = \| - j\mu\delta_{ij} \|$ and thus

$$\mathbf{P}(t) = \mathbf{H} \| e^{-j\mu t}\delta_{ij} \| \mathbf{H}$$

or

$$P_{ik}(t) = \sum_{j=0}^{\infty} \alpha_{ij}\alpha_{jk}e^{-j\mu t}.$$

We can easily obtain

$$\sum_{k=0}^{\infty} P_{ik}(t)z^k = e^{-\frac{\lambda}{\mu}(1-z)(1-e^{-\mu t})}[1 - (1 - z)e^{-\mu t}]^i$$

and hence

$$\lim_{t \to \infty} P_{ik}(t) = P_k = \frac{e^{-\lambda/\mu}}{k!}\left(\frac{\lambda}{u}\right)^k.$$

23. The process $\{\xi_t\}$ is now a homogeneous Markov process. If $\xi_t = n$, then we say that the system is in state E_n at time t. Now $c_n = n\lambda$, $p_{n, n+1} = 1$ and by (20) the following system of differential equations holds:

$$\frac{dP_n(t)}{dt} = -n\lambda P_n(t) + (n-1)\lambda P_{n-1}(t), \qquad (n = 1, 2, \ldots).$$

The initial conditions are

$$P_n(0) = \begin{cases} 1 & \text{if} \quad n = 1, \\ 0 & \text{if} \quad n \neq 1. \end{cases}$$

The solution is

$$P_n(t) = e^{-\lambda t}(1 - e^{-\lambda t})^{n-1}, \qquad (n = 1, 2, \ldots).$$

If the initial conditions are

$$P_n(0) = \begin{cases} 1 & \text{if} \quad n = m, \\ 0 & \text{if} \quad n \neq m, \end{cases}$$

then the solution is

$$P_n(t) = \binom{n-1}{m-1} e^{-m\lambda t}(1 - e^{-\lambda t})^{n-m}.$$

24. The process in question is a homogeneous Markov process with $c_n = \lambda_n$ and $p_{n, n+1} = 1$. Thus by (20) we have

$$(*) \qquad \frac{dP_n(t)}{dt} = -\lambda_n P_n(t) + \lambda_{n-1} P_{n-1}(t), \qquad (n = 0, 1, 2, \ldots),$$

where the initial conditions are

$$P_n(0) = \begin{cases} 1 & \text{if} \quad n = 0, \\ 0 & \text{if} \quad n \neq 0. \end{cases}$$

If the numbers λ_n are different, then the solution is

$$P_n(t) = (-1)^n \lambda_0 \lambda_1 \ldots \lambda_{n-1} \sum_{k=0}^{n} \frac{e^{-\lambda_k t}}{\displaystyle\prod_{j=0}^{n}{}'(\lambda_k - \lambda_j)},$$

where the factor of the product which corresponds to $j = k$ is missing.

Let $S_k(t) = P_0(t) + P_1(t) + \ldots + P_k(t)$, then (∗) implies that
$$S_k'(t) = - \lambda_k P_k(t),$$
and thus

$$1 - S_k(t) = \lambda_k \int_0^t P_k(u)\, du, \quad \text{if} \quad k \geq 0.$$

Since $S_k(t)$, $(k = 0, 1, 2, \ldots)$ is a monotone non-decreasing sequence, therefore $\lambda_k \int_0^t P_k(u)\, du$ is a monotone non-increasing sequence of non-negative numbers which converge to a limit $P^*(t)$. Hence

$$P^*(t) \leq \lambda_k \int_0^t P_k(u)\, du.$$

Consequently

$$\left(\frac{1}{\lambda_0} + \frac{1}{\lambda_1} + \ldots + \frac{1}{\lambda_n} \right) P^*(t) \leq \int_0^t S_n(u)\, du \leq \left(\frac{1}{\lambda_0} + \frac{1}{\lambda_1} + \ldots + \frac{1}{\lambda_n} \right),$$

and since $S_n(t) \leq 1$ for all n, therefore

$$P^*(t) \sum_{n=0}^{\infty} \frac{1}{\lambda_n} \leq t.$$

If now $\sum_{n=0}^{\infty} \frac{1}{\lambda_n} = \infty$, then we must have $P^*(t) = 0$, that is,
$\lim_{t \to \infty} S_n(t) \equiv 1$. If, however, $\sum_{n=0}^{\infty} \frac{1}{\lambda_n} < \infty$, then $\int_0^t S_n(u)\, du < \infty$
and therefore $\lim_{t \to \infty} S_n(t) = 1$ cannot hold for all t.

25. The process $\{\xi_t\}$ is a homogeneous Markov process with $c_n = n(\lambda + \mu)$, $c_n p_{n, n+1} = n\lambda$, $c_n p_{n, n-1} = n\mu$. Now by (20) we have

$$\frac{dP_n(t)}{dt} = - n(\lambda + \mu) P_n(t) + (n - 1)\lambda P_{n-1}(t) + (n + 1)\mu P_{n+1}(t)$$

and the initial conditions are

$$P_n(0) = \begin{cases} 1 & \text{if} \quad n = 1, \\ 0 & \text{f} \quad n \neq 1. \end{cases}$$

Let us introduce the generating function:

$$U(t, z) = \sum_{n=0}^{\infty} P_n(t)z^n.$$

This satisfies the partial differential equation:

$$\frac{\partial U}{\partial t} = (\lambda z - \mu)(z - 1)\frac{\partial U}{\partial z}$$

and the initial condition is $U(0, z) = z$.

The solution is

$$U(z) = \frac{\mu\sigma + z[1 - (\lambda + \mu)\sigma]}{1 - z\lambda\sigma},$$

where

$$\sigma = \begin{cases} \dfrac{1 - e^{(\lambda-\mu)t}}{\mu - \lambda e^{(\lambda-\mu)t}} & \text{if } \lambda \neq \mu, \\[2ex] \dfrac{t}{1 + \mu t} & \text{if } \lambda = \mu. \end{cases}$$

Hence $\begin{cases} P_0(t) = \mu\sigma, \\ P_n(t) = (1 - \lambda\sigma)(1 - \mu\sigma)(\lambda\sigma)^{n-1}, \end{cases}$ $(n = 1, 2, \ldots).$

Finally

$$\lim_{t \to \infty} P_0(t) = \begin{cases} 1 & \text{if } \mu \geqq \lambda, \\ \mu/\lambda & \text{if } \mu \leqq \lambda. \end{cases}$$

26. The process $\{\xi_t\}$ is an inhomogeneous Markov process with

$$c_n(t) = n\lambda + n\mu t, \quad p_{n, n+1}(t) = n\lambda/(n\lambda + n\mu t),$$
$$p_{n, n+1}(t) = n\mu t/(n\lambda + n\mu t).$$

By (14) we have

$$\frac{dP_n(t)}{dt} = -(n\lambda + n\mu t)P_n(t) + (n - 1)\lambda P_{n-1}(t) + (n + 1)\mu t P_{n+1}(t)$$
$$(n = 0, 1, 2, \ldots)$$

and the initial conditions are

$$P_n(0) = \begin{cases} 1 & \text{if } n = 1, \\ 0 & \text{if } n \neq 1. \end{cases}$$

By applying the method of generating functions we get the following solution:

$$P_0(t) = 1 - \frac{e^{\frac{\lambda^2}{2\mu}}}{\left[A + e^{\frac{(\mu t - \lambda)^2}{2\mu}}\right]}, \qquad P_n(t) = \frac{A^{n-1}e^{-\lambda t + \frac{\mu}{2}t^2 + \frac{\lambda^2}{\mu}}}{\left[A + e^{\frac{(\mu t - \lambda)^2}{2\mu}}\right]^{n+1}},$$

where

$$A = \lambda \int_0^t e^{\frac{(\mu s - \lambda)^2}{2\mu}} ds.$$

27. By (14) we have

$$\frac{dP_n(t)}{dt} = -\frac{1 + nd}{1 + td}P_n(t) + \frac{1 + (n-1)d}{1 + td}P_{n-1}(t),$$
$$(n = 0, 1, 2, \ldots).$$

The initial conditions are

$$P_n(0) = \begin{cases} 1 & \text{if} \quad n = 0, \\ 0 & \text{if} \quad n \neq 0. \end{cases}$$

The solution is

$$P_0(t) = \left(\frac{1}{1 + dt}\right)^{1/d},$$

$$P_n(t) = \left(\frac{1}{1 + dt}\right)^{1/d}\left(\frac{t}{1 + dt}\right)^n \frac{(1 + d)(1 + 2d) \ldots (1 + (n-1)d)}{n!}.$$

28. It follows from (29) that $f(s, y; t, x)$ satisfies the so-called heat conduction equation

$$\frac{\partial f(s, y; t, x)}{\partial t} = \frac{1}{2} \frac{\partial^2 f(s, y; t, x)}{\partial x^2},$$

the solution of which is

$$f(s, y; t, x) = \sqrt{\frac{1}{2\pi(t - s)}} \, e^{-\frac{(x-y)^2}{2(t-s)}}.$$

In this case we say that the process $\{\xi\}$ is a *Gaussian process*.

29. According to (29) we have to solve the following equation:

$$\frac{\partial f(s, y; t, x)}{\partial t} + a(t)\frac{\partial f(s, y; t, x)}{\partial x} = \frac{b(t)}{2} \frac{\partial^2 f(s, y; t, x)}{\partial x^2}.$$

Let us introduce new coordinates

$$x' = x - \int_a^t a(u)\,du, \qquad y' = y - \int_a^s a(u)\,du,$$

$$t' = \int_a^t b(u)\,du, \qquad s' = \int_a^s b(u)\,du,$$

then we obtain

$$\frac{\partial f}{\partial t'} = \frac{1}{2}\,\frac{\partial^2 f}{\partial x'^2}$$

and the solution of this is

$$f(s, y; t, x) = \sqrt{\frac{1}{2\pi(t'-s')}}\,e^{-\frac{(x'-y')^2}{2(t'-s')}} = \sqrt{\frac{1}{2\pi\beta}}\,e^{-\frac{(x-\alpha)^2}{2\beta}}$$

where

$$\beta = \int_s^t b(u)\,du \quad \text{and} \quad \alpha = y + \int_s^t a(u)\,du.$$

30. Let now $\mathbf{P}\{\xi_t \le x \mid \xi_0 = 0\} = F(0, 0; t, x) = F(t, x)$. In the notation of Section 6, $p(t, x) = \lambda$, $P(t, y; x) = U(x - y)$, and there is no continuous transition. It follows from (36) that

$$\frac{\partial F(t, x)}{\partial t} = -\lambda[F(t, x) - \int_0^x U(x - y)d_y F(t, y)]$$

and the initial condition is

$$F(0, x) = \begin{cases} 1 & \text{if } x \ge 0, \\ 0 & \text{if } x < 0. \end{cases}$$

The solution is

$$F(t, x) = \sum_{n=0}^{\infty} e^{-\lambda t}\frac{(\lambda t)^n}{n!}\,U_n(x),$$

where $U_n(x)$ is the n-th iterated convolution of $U(x)$ with itself. $U_0(x) = 1$ if $x \ge 0$, $U_0(x) = 0$ if $x < 0$, $U_1(x) = U(x)$ and $U_n(x)$ $(n = 2, 3, \ldots)$ can be determined by the recurrence formula

$$U_n(x) = \int_0^x U_{n-1}(x - y)\,dU(y).$$

31. Let $\mathbf{P}\{\xi_t \le x \mid \xi_0 = 0\} = F(0, 0; t, x) = F(t, x)$. The process $\{\xi_t\}$ is a Markov process with $p(t, x) = \lambda$, $P(t, y, x) = H(x - y)$ and

$$G(t, y; t + \Delta t, x) = \begin{cases} 1 & \text{if } x > ye^{-\alpha\Delta t}, \\ 0 & \text{if } x \le ye^{-\alpha\Delta t}, \end{cases}$$

that is, $a(t, x) = -x\alpha$, $b(t, x) = 0$. By (36) we have

$$(*) \quad \frac{\partial F(t, x)}{\partial t} = x\alpha \frac{\partial F(t, x)}{\partial x} - \lambda[F(t, x) - \int_0^x H(x - y)d_y F(t, y)]$$

and

$$F(0, x) = \begin{cases} 1 & \text{if } x \ge 0, \\ 0 & \text{if } x < 0. \end{cases}$$

If the limiting distribution $\lim_{t \to \infty} F(t, x) = F(x)$ exists, then by $(*)$, it will satisfy the following equation

$$F'(x) = \frac{\lambda}{\alpha x} [F(x) - \int_0^x H(x - y) \, dF(y)].$$

However, there is an easier method of determining the distribution function $F(t, x)$. Let u be a fixed time instant and consider the process $\{\eta_t\}$ where $\eta_t = \xi_u - \xi_{u-t}$. The process $\{\eta_t\}$ is also a Markov process. Although it is not homogeneous it will be additive, whereas $\{\xi_t\}$ was not, and its transitions will be accomplished exclusively through jumps. Obviously $\mathbf{P}\{\eta_t \le x\} = F(t, x)$ and with the notation of Section 6, $p(t, x) = \lambda$ and $P(t, y, x) = H[(x - y)e^{\alpha t}]$. From (36) it follows that

$$(**) \quad \frac{\partial F(t, x)}{\partial t} = -\lambda \left\{ F(t, x) - \int_0^x H[(x - y)e^{\alpha t}]d_y F(t, y) \right\},$$

which is a simpler equation for determining $F(t, x)$ than $(*)$. The method of characteristic functions is applicable to solve $(**)$. Let

$$\Phi(t, z) = \int_0^\infty e^{izx}d_x F(t, x), \qquad \psi(z) = \int_0^\infty e^{izx} \, dH(x),$$

then it follows from $(**)$ that

$$\frac{\partial \Phi(t, z)}{\partial t} = -\lambda[1 - \psi(ze^{-\alpha t})]\Phi(t, z),$$

the solution of which is

$$\Phi(t, z) = \exp\left\{ -\lambda \int_0^t [1 - \psi(ze^{-\alpha u})]\, du \right\}.$$

$F(t, x)$ can be uniquely determined by inverting its characteristic function $\Phi(t, z)$.

Under the assumption that $\displaystyle\int_0^\infty x\, dH(x) < \infty$ we can easily show that the limit $\displaystyle\lim_{t \to \infty} \Phi(t, z) = \Phi(z)$ exists and is continuous at $z = 0$. In this case it follows from the well-known theorem of *P. Lévy* and *H. Cramér* about the convergence of characteristic functions that $\displaystyle\lim_{\to \infty} F(t, x) = F(x)$ also exists and $\Phi(z)$ is the characteristic function of $F(x)$. Now

$$\Phi(z) = \exp\left\{ -\frac{\lambda}{\alpha} \int_0^1 \frac{1 - \psi(zx)}{x}\, dx \right\},$$

and $F(x)$ can be uniquely determined by inverting $\Phi(z)$. Hitherto we have proved that

$$\lim_{t \to \infty} \mathbf{P}\{\xi_t \leq x \mid \xi_0 = 0\} = F(x).$$

If $\xi_0 = y$, then

$$\mathbf{P}\{\xi_t \leq x \mid \xi_0 = y\} = \mathbf{P}\{\xi_t \leq x - ye^{-\alpha t} \mid \xi_0 = 0\}$$

and consequently we have

$$\lim_{t \to \infty} \mathbf{P}\{\xi_t \leq x \mid \xi_0 = y\} = F(x)$$

in every continuity point of $F(x)$.

32. The process $\{\xi_t\}$ is a Markov process whose transitions are accomplished both continuously and by jumps. With the notation of Section 6,

$$p(t, x) = \lambda, \qquad P(t, y, x) = H(x - y)$$

and

$$G(t, y; t + \Delta t, x) = \begin{cases} 1 & \text{if } x \geq y - \Delta t, \\ 0 & \text{if } x < y - \Delta t, \end{cases}$$

if $y > 0$. Thus $a(t, x) = -1$ and $b(t, x) = 0$ if $x > 0$. Let $\mathbf{P}\{\xi_t \leq x \mid \xi_0 = 0\} = F(t, x)$, then, according to (36),

$$\frac{\partial F(t, x)}{\partial t} = \frac{\partial F(t, x)}{\partial x} - \lambda\left[F(t, x) - \int_0^\infty H(x - y)d_y F(t, y)\right]$$

for $x > 0$. By introducing the Laplace-Stieltjes transforms

$$\Phi(t, s) = \int_0^\infty e^{-sx} d_x F(t, x), \qquad \psi(s) = \int_0^\infty e^{-sx} dH(x)$$

we obtain

$$(*) \qquad \frac{\partial \Phi(t, s)}{\partial t} = \Phi(t, s)[s - \lambda + \lambda\psi(s)] - sF(t, 0).$$

Let $\alpha = \int_0^\infty x \, dH(x)$ and suppose $\lambda\alpha < 1$. It can be shown that $\lim_{t \to \infty} \Phi(t, s) = \Phi(s)$ exists and is continuous at $s = 0$. In this case the limiting distribution $\lim_{t \to \infty} F(t, x) = F(x)$ also exists and $\Phi(s) = \int_0^\infty e^{-sx} dF(x)$. It follows from $(*)$ that

$$\Phi(s) = \frac{sF(0)}{s - \lambda + \lambda\psi(s)}.$$

Since $\Phi(0) = 1$ and $\psi'(0) = -\alpha$ therefore $F(0) = 1 - \lambda\alpha$ and finally

$$\Phi(s) = \frac{1 - \lambda\alpha}{1 - \lambda\dfrac{1 - \psi(s)}{s}}.$$

The distribution function $F(x)$ can be obtained uniquely by inverse transformation of $\Phi(s)$.

33. The process $\{\xi_t\}$ is an additive Markov process whose transitions are accomplished exclusively by jumps. With the notation of Section 6 $p(t, x) = \lambda e^{-x/2}$ and $P(t, y, x) = H(x - y)$ where

$$H(x) = \frac{\lambda_1 H_1(x) + \ldots + \lambda_r H_r(x)}{\lambda_1 + \ldots + \lambda_r}.$$

and $\lambda = \lambda_1 + \ldots + \lambda_r$. Let $\mathbf{P}\{\xi_t \leq x \mid \xi_0 = 0\} = F(t, x)$, then it follows from (36) that

$$(*) \qquad \frac{\partial F(t, x)}{\partial t} = - \lambda \int_0^x [1 - H(x - y)] e^{-\frac{y}{2}} d_y F(t, y),$$

and the initial condition is

$$F(0, x) = \begin{cases} 1 & \text{if} \quad x \geqq 0, \\ 0 & \text{if} \quad x < 0. \end{cases}$$

The equation $(*)$ can be solved by Laplace–Stieltjes transformation. Let

$$\Phi(t, s) = \int_0^\infty e^{-sx} d_x F(t, x), \qquad \psi(s) = \int_0^\infty e^{-sx} dH(x),$$

then

$$\frac{\partial \Phi(t, s)}{\partial t} = - \lambda [1 - \psi(s)] \Phi(t, s + \tfrac{1}{2}).$$

Since $\Phi(0, s) = 1$, therefore

$$\Phi(t, s) = 1 - \lambda [1 - \psi(s)] \int_0^t \Phi(u, s + \tfrac{1}{2}) \, du.$$

By repeated applications of this formula $\Phi(t, s)$ can be expressed consecutively in terms of $\Phi(t, s + \tfrac{1}{2}n)$, $(n = 1, 2, 3, \ldots)$. Noting that

$$\lim_{n \to \infty} \Phi\left(t, s + \frac{n}{2}\right) = 0$$

we finally obtain

$$\Phi(t, s) = \sum_{n=0}^\infty \frac{(-1)^n (\lambda t)^n}{n!} \prod_{j=0}^{n-1} \left[1 - \psi\left(s + \frac{j}{2}\right)\right].$$

and $F(t, x)$ can be determined uniquely by inversion. Now $\mathbf{E}\{E_t\} = \mathbf{E}\{E_0 e^{-\xi_t}\} = E_0 \Phi(t, 1)$, i.e.

$$\mathbf{E}\{E_t\} = E_0 \sum_{n=0}^\infty \frac{(-1)^n (\lambda t)^n}{n!} \prod_{j=0}^{n-1} \left[1 - \psi\left(1 + \frac{j}{2}\right)\right].$$

34. Let us say that the component is in state E_1 if the machine is working, in state E_2 if the machine is not working and in state E_3

if it has failed. Let $P_1(t)$, $P_2(t)$, $P_3(t)$ be the corresponding probabilities at time t. The initial conditions are $P_1(0) = 1$, $P_2(0) = P_3(0) = 0$. According to (20) we have

$$P_1'(t) = -(\lambda + \gamma)P_1(t) + \eta P_2(t),$$
$$P_2'(t) = \gamma P_1(t) - \eta P_2(t),$$
$$P_3'(t) = \lambda P_1(t),$$

and

$$F(t) = P_3(t) = \lambda \int_0^t P_1(u)\, du.$$

The characteristic equation of the system formed from the first two equations is

$$\begin{vmatrix} -(\lambda + \gamma + \omega) & \eta \\ \gamma & -(\eta + \omega) \end{vmatrix} = \omega^2 + (\eta + \lambda + \gamma)\omega + \lambda\eta = 0,$$

and the roots of this equation are

$$\omega_1, \omega_2 = \frac{-(\eta + \lambda + \gamma) \pm \sqrt{(\eta + \lambda + \gamma)^2 - 4\lambda\eta}}{2}.$$

Thereby we can obtain easily that

$$P_1(t) = \frac{\eta + \omega_1}{\omega_1 - \omega_2} e^{\omega_1 t} - \frac{\eta + \omega_2}{\omega_1 - \omega_2} e^{\omega_2 t},$$

from which $F(t)$ can be calculated. Now $-\infty < \omega_2 < -\eta < \omega_1 < 0$ and since $F'(t) = \lambda P_1(t)$, therefore

$$m = \int_0^\infty t\, dF(t) = \frac{\eta + \lambda}{\eta\lambda}$$

$$\sigma^2 = \int_0^\infty (t - m)^2\, dF(t) = \left(\frac{\eta + \lambda}{\eta\lambda}\right)^2 + \frac{2\lambda\gamma}{\lambda^2\eta^2}.$$

3. Non-Markovian processes

1. The conditional expectation of ξ_t given that $\tau_1 = y$ is

$$\mathbf{E}\{\xi_t \mid \tau_1 = y\} = \begin{cases} 1 + m(t - y) & \text{if } y \leq t, \\ 0 & \text{if } y > t, \end{cases}$$

and therefore by the theorem of total expectation we have

$$\mathbf{E}\{\xi_t\} = \int_0^\infty \mathbf{E}\{\xi_t \mid \tau_1 = y\}\, dF(y),$$

i.e.

$$m(t) = F(t) + \int_0^t m(t - y)\, dF(y).$$

$m(t)$ can be obtained by the solution of this integral equation. Forming the Laplace–Stieltjes transform of this equation we obtain

$$\int_0^\infty e^{-st}\, dm(t) = \phi(s) + \phi(s) \int_0^\infty e^{-st}\, dm(t),$$

which implies (5).

2. $m(t)$ is a monotone non-decreasing function and

$$\mu(s) = \int_0^\infty e^{-st}\, dm(t) = \frac{\phi(s)}{1 - \phi(s)}.$$

Now

$$\lim_{s \to 0} \frac{s\phi(s)}{1 - \phi(s)} = \frac{-1}{\phi'(0)} = \frac{1}{\mu}$$

and therefore

$$\lim_{t \to \infty} \frac{m(t)}{t} = \frac{1}{\mu}.$$

3. $\mathbf{P}\{\xi_t < n\} = \mathbf{P}\{t < \tau_n\}$ holds for arbitrary $t \geq 0$ and $n \geq 0$. Let

$$n = \left[\frac{t}{\mu} + x \sqrt{\frac{\sigma^2 t}{\mu^3}}\right],$$

where $[a]$ means the integral part of a. Obviously

$$\mathbf{P}\{\xi_t < n\} = \mathbf{P}\left\{\frac{\xi_t - t/\mu}{\sqrt{\sigma^2 t/\mu^3}} < \frac{n - t/\mu}{\sqrt{\sigma^2 t/\mu^3}}\right\}$$

and since

$$\lim_{t \to \infty} \frac{n - t/\mu}{\sqrt{\sigma^2 t/\mu^3}} = x,$$

therefore

$$(*) \qquad \lim_{t \to \infty} \mathbf{P}\{\xi_t < n\} = \lim_{t \to \infty} \mathbf{P}\left\{\frac{\xi_t - t/\mu}{\sqrt{\sigma^2 t/\mu^3}} < x\right\}$$

at each continuity point of the limiting distribution. On the other hand,

$$\mathbf{P}\{t < \tau_n\} = \mathbf{P}\left\{\frac{t - n\mu}{\sqrt{n\sigma^2}} < \frac{\tau_n - n\mu}{\sqrt{n\sigma^2}}\right\}$$

and

$$\lim_{t \to \infty} \frac{t - n\mu}{\sqrt{n\sigma^2}} = -x,$$

hence it follows from the central limit theorem that

$$(**) \quad \lim_{t \to \infty} \mathbf{P}\{t < \tau_n\} = \lim_{n \to \infty} \mathbf{P}\left\{-x < \frac{\tau_n - n\mu}{\sqrt{n\sigma^2}}\right\}$$
$$= \frac{1}{\sqrt{2\pi}} \int_{-x}^{\infty} e^{-\frac{1}{2}u^2} \, du = \frac{1}{\sqrt{2\pi}} \int_{-\infty}^{x} e^{-\frac{1}{2}u^2} \, du.$$

The identity of $(*)$ and $(**)$ proves the theorem.

4. It is obviously true that

$$\mathbf{P}\{\xi_{u+t} - \xi_u \le n\} = 1 - \mathbf{P}\{\eta_u \le t\} * F_n(t)$$

and under the present assumptions

$$\lim_{u \to \infty} \mathbf{P}\{\eta_u \le t\} = F^*(t).$$

5. We can easily see that

$$\mathbf{P}\{\eta_t{}^* \le x\} = \int_0^x [1 - F(x - u)] \frac{m(t + u) - m(u)}{t} \, du.$$

If $\mu < \infty$ then $\lim_{t \to \infty} \dfrac{m(t)}{t} = \dfrac{1}{\mu}$ and consequently

$$\lim_{t \to \infty} \mathbf{P}\{\eta_t^* \le x\} = F^*(x).$$

6. Obviously

$$\mathbf{P}\{\xi_{\tau+t} - \xi_\tau \le n\} = 1 - \mathbf{P}\{\eta_T^* \le t\} * F_n(t)$$

and $\lim_{T \to \infty} \mathbf{P}\{\eta_T^* \le t\} = F^*(t), \qquad \text{if } \mu < \infty.$

7. Consider the random variable τ_ν, where $\nu = \xi_t + 1$. Here $\tau_\nu = \tau_1 + (\tau_2 - \tau_1) + \ldots + (\tau_\nu - \tau_{\nu-1})$ and the event $\nu = n$ is independent of the random variables $(\tau_{n+1} - \tau_n), (\tau_{n+2} - \tau_{n+1}), \ldots$ By applying *A. Wald's* well-known theorem we obtain that $\mathbf{E}\{\tau_\nu\} = \mathbf{E}\{\nu\}\mathbf{E}\{\tau_1\}$. Since $\tau_\nu = t + \eta_t$ and $\nu = \xi_t + 1$, therefore $t + \mathbf{E}\{\eta_t\} = [m(t) + 1]\mu$, i.e.

$$m(t) - \frac{t}{\mu} = \frac{\mathbf{E}\{\eta_t\}}{\mu} - 1$$

and under the stated conditions

$$\lim_{\to \infty} \mathbf{E}\{\eta_t\} = \frac{\sigma^2 + \mu^2}{2\mu}.$$

8. We have $\vartheta_t \leq x$ if and only if there occurs at least one event during $(t - x, t]$ and if the last amongst them is the n-th event then $\tau_{n+1} - \tau_n \leq x$. (In this case evidently $t < \tau_{n+1}$.) Then by the theorem of total probability we have

$$\mathbf{P}\{\vartheta_t \leq x\} = \sum_{n=1}^{\infty} \int_{t-x}^{t} [F(x) - F(t - u)]dF_n(u)$$

$$= \int_{t-x}^{t} [F(x) - F(t - u)]dm(u)$$

if $t > x$ and hence

$$\lim_{t \to \infty} \mathbf{P}\{\vartheta_t \leq x\} = \frac{1}{\mu} \int_0^x [F(x) - F(y)]dy = \frac{1}{\mu} \int_0^x y \, dF(y),$$

for $x \geq 0$.

It can be shown further that

$$\lim_{t \to \infty} \mathbf{E}\{\vartheta_t\} = \frac{1}{\mu} \int_0^{\infty} x^2 \, dF(x) = \mu + \frac{\sigma^2}{\mu}.$$

9. The sequence of renewal times form a recurrent process. The problem is to find $m(t)$ where

$$\mu(s) = \int_0^{\infty} e^{-st} \, dm(t) = \frac{\phi(s)}{1 - \phi(s)}.$$

In this case $\phi(s) = [\lambda/(\lambda + s)]^m$ and therefore

$$\mu(s) = \frac{1}{\left(1 + \dfrac{s}{\lambda}\right)^m - 1}.$$

Let $\varepsilon_r = e^{\frac{2\pi r i}{m}}$ $(r = 0, 1, \ldots, m - 1)$. Then we can express $\mu(s)$ in terms of partial fractions as follows:

$$\mu(s) = \frac{1}{m} \sum_{r=0}^{m-1} \frac{\lambda \varepsilon_r}{s + \lambda(1 - \varepsilon_r)}$$

and hence

$$m(t) = \frac{\lambda t}{m} + \frac{1}{m} \sum_{r=1}^{m-1} \frac{\varepsilon_r}{1 - \varepsilon_r} [1 - e^{-\lambda t(1 - \varepsilon_r)}].$$

On the other hand, we have

$$\mu(s) = \sum_{j=1}^{\infty} \left(\frac{\lambda}{\lambda + s}\right)^{mj}$$

and consequently

$$m'(t) = e^{-\lambda t} \lambda \sum_{j=1}^{\infty} \frac{(\lambda t)^{mj-1}}{(mj - 1)!}$$

holds also.

10. We have $\mathbf{P}\{\xi_t \leqq n\} = 1 - \hat{F}(t) * F_n(t)$. Thus

$$m(t) = \mathbf{E}\{\xi_t\} = \sum_{n=0}^{\infty} \hat{F}(t) * F_n(t)$$

and

$$\int_0^{\infty} e^{-st} dm(t) = \sum_{n=0}^{\infty} \hat{\phi}(s)[\phi(s)]^n = \frac{\hat{\phi}(s)}{1 - \phi(s)}.$$

11. Let $\tau_1, \tau_2, \ldots, \tau_n, \ldots$ denote the instants of registrations. The time differences $\tau_n - \tau_{n-1} (n = 1, 2, 3, \ldots; \tau_0 = 0)$ are independent random variables; $\mathbf{P}\{\tau_1 \leqq x\} = 1 - e^{-\lambda x}$ if $x \geqq 0$, and $\tau_n - \tau_{n-1}$

$(n = 2, 3, \ldots)$ are identically distributed with distribution function $F(x)$ which is not known at present. Denote by $m(t)$ the expected number of registrations during $(0, t]$ and let

$$\phi(s) = \int_0^\infty e^{-sx} \, dF(x).$$

According to Problem 10 we can write

$$\int_0^\infty e^{-st} \, dm(t) = \frac{\lambda}{\lambda + s} \frac{1}{1 - \phi(s)}$$

and consequently

$$\phi(s) = 1 - \frac{\lambda}{\lambda + s} \left[\int_0^\infty e^{-st} \, dm(t) \right]^{-1}.$$

Here $m'(t) = e^{-\lambda t}\lambda$ if $t < \alpha$, and $m'(t) = e^{-\lambda \alpha}\lambda$ if $t \geq \alpha$. For $m(t + \Delta t) - m(t) = e^{-\lambda t}\lambda\Delta t + o(\Delta t)$ if $t < \alpha$, and $m(t + \Delta t) - m(t) = e^{-\lambda \alpha}\lambda\Delta t + o(\Delta t)$ if $t \geq \alpha$ since a particle is registered in the time interval $(t, t + \Delta t)$ if no particle arrives during $(t - \alpha, t)$, but one arrives in the time interval $(t, t + \Delta t)$. If $\Delta t < \alpha$ then at most one registration can occur in $(t, t + \Delta t)$. Thus

$$\int_0^\infty e^{-st} \, dm(t) = \frac{\lambda}{\lambda + s} \left(\frac{s + \lambda e^{-(\lambda + s)\alpha}}{s} \right)$$

and thereby

$$\phi(s) = \frac{\lambda e^{-\alpha(\lambda + s)}}{s + \lambda e^{-\alpha(\lambda + s)}}.$$

By inversion we find for $x \geq 0$ that

$$F(x) = \sum_{j=1}^{[x/\alpha]} (-1)^{j-1} \frac{e^{-\lambda \alpha j}\lambda^j}{j!} (x - j\alpha)^j.$$

If ξ_t denotes the number of registrations in the time interval $(0, t)$ and $\mathbf{P}\{\xi_t \leq n\} = W(t, n)$, then

$$s \int_0^\infty e^{-st} W(t, n) \, dt = 1 - \frac{\lambda}{\lambda + s} [\phi(s)]^n$$

and we obtain by inversion that

$$W(t, n) = 1 - (-1)^{n-1} \sum_{j=n}^{[t/\alpha]} \binom{j-1}{n-1} e^{-j\lambda\alpha}$$

$$\cdot \left[e^{-\lambda(t-j\alpha)} - \sum_{k=0}^{j} (-1)^k \frac{\lambda^k (t-j\alpha)^k}{k!} \right].$$

According to (19) the stationary distribution $W^*(t, n)$ can be obtained as follows:

$$W^*(t, n) = 1 - \sum_{j=n}^{[t/\alpha]} (-1)^{j-n} \binom{j}{n} \frac{e^{-\lambda\alpha(j+1)}\lambda^{j+1}(t-j\alpha)^{j+1}}{(j+1)!}.$$

The mean value of $F(x)$ is $\mu = e^{\lambda\alpha}/\lambda$ while its variance

$$\sigma^2 = e^{\lambda\alpha}(e^{\lambda\alpha} - 2\lambda\alpha)/\lambda^2.$$

It follows from Problem 3 that the distribution of ξ_t is asymptotically normal with mean value t/μ and variance $\sigma^2 t/\mu^3$.

12. Denote by $\{\tau_n\}$ the sequence of the instants of registration. As in Problem 11, the time differences $\tau_n - \tau_{n-1}$ $(n = 1, 2, 3, \ldots; \tau_0 = 0)$ are independent random variables, given by

$$\mathbf{P}\{\tau_1 \leq x\} = 1 - e^{-\lambda x}$$

if $x \geq 0$ and $\tau_n - \tau_{n-1}$ $(n = 2, 3, \ldots)$ identically distributed random variables with distribution function $F(x) = 1 - e^{-\lambda(x-\alpha)}$ (if $x \geq \alpha$) and $F(x) = 0$ (if $x < \alpha$). Now

$$\phi(s) = \int_0^\infty e^{-sx} \, dF(x) = \frac{\lambda e^{-s\alpha}}{\lambda + s}$$

and the argument for solving Problem 11 can be repeated with this function $\phi(s)$. Thus

$$W(t, n) = \begin{cases} \displaystyle\sum_{j=0}^{n} e^{-\lambda(t-n\alpha)} \frac{\lambda^j(t-n\alpha)^j}{j!} & \text{if } n\alpha \leq t, \\ \\ 1 & \text{if } n\alpha \geq t. \end{cases}$$

At present $\mu = (1 + \lambda\alpha)/\lambda$ is the mean value and $\sigma^2 = 1/\lambda^2$ is the variance of $F(x)$ and the number of registered particles during

$(0, t]$ has an asymptotically normal distribution with mean value t/μ and variance $\sigma^2 t/\mu^3$.

13. Problems 11 and 12 are special cases of the present problem for $p = 1$ and $p = 0$ respectively. Let $\tau_1, \tau_2, \ldots, \tau_n, \ldots$ denote the instants of registration. The random variables $\tau_n - \tau_{n-1}(n = 1, 2, 3, \ldots; \tau_0 = 0)$ are independent. Now

$$\mathbf{P}\{\tau_1 \le x\} = 1 - e^{-\lambda x} \quad (x \ge 0)$$

and the time differences $\tau_n - \tau_{n-1}$ $(n = 2, 3, \ldots)$ are identically distributed, but their distribution function $F(x)$ is unknown at present. Let

$$\phi(s) = \int_0^\infty e^{-sx}\, dF(x)$$

and denote by $m(t)$ the expectation of the number of registrations during $(\tau_1, \tau_1 + t]$, where the first registration is taken to be the starting point for time measurements. If

$$\mu(s) = \int_0^\infty e^{-st}\, dm(t)$$

then by (25) we have $\phi(s) = \mu(s)/[1 + \mu(s)]$. Denote by $G(t)$ the probability that the first particle after τ_1 which gives rise to an impulse arrives during time t. For this probability we can write that

$$G(t) = \begin{cases} 1 - e^{-\lambda p t} & \text{if } 0 \le t < \alpha, \\ 1 - e^{-\lambda t + \lambda \alpha(1-p)} & \text{if } \alpha \le t < \infty. \end{cases}$$

We have $m(t) = 0$ if $t < \alpha$ and

$$m(t) = G(t) - G(\alpha) + \int_0^t m(t - y)\, dG(y)$$

if $t \ge \alpha$, which can be proved by the theorem of total expectation. Converting to Laplace–Stieltjes transforms we obtain

$$\mu(s) = \int_\alpha^\infty e^{-st}\, dG(t) \bigg/ \left\{ 1 - \int_0^\infty e^{-st}\, dG(t) \right\}$$

and thus

$$\phi(s) = \int_\alpha^\infty e^{-st}\, dG(t) \bigg/ \left\{ 1 - \int_0^\alpha e^{-st}\, dG(t) \right\}$$

or

$$\phi(s) = \frac{\lambda p + s}{\lambda p + sp} \left(\frac{\lambda p e^{-(\lambda p + s)\alpha}}{s + \lambda p e^{-(\lambda p + s)\alpha}} \right).$$

$F(x)$ can be determined uniquely from $\phi(s)$ by inversion. If μ is the mean value and σ^2 the variance of $F(x)$, then the number of registered particles in the time interval $(0, t]$ has an asymptotically normal distribution as $t \longrightarrow \infty$ with mean value t/μ and variance $\sigma^2 t/\mu^3$ where

$$\mu = \frac{e^{\lambda p \alpha} + p - 1}{\lambda p}, \qquad \sigma^2 = \frac{e^{\lambda p \alpha}(e^{\lambda p \alpha} - 2\lambda p \alpha) + p^2 - 1}{(\lambda p)^2}.$$

The density of registration is $f = 1/\mu$.

14. The solution method of Problem 11 can be applied word for word, only the distribution function $F(x)$ will now be different. In this case we have similarly

$$\phi(s) = 1 - \frac{\lambda}{\lambda + s} \left[\int_0^\infty e^{-st} \, dm(t) \right]^{-1},$$

but now

$$m'(t) = \lambda \exp \left\{ - \lambda \int_0^t [1 - H(x)] \, dx \right\}.$$

This can be proved as follows: Denote by $P_0(t)$ the probability that there is no impulse in progress at time t. This event will occur if all impulses starting during $(0, t]$ will end before the instant t. Using the well-known property of the Poisson process (Chapter 2, Problem 7), we can write by the theorem of total probability that

$$P_0(t) = \sum_{n=0}^\infty e^{-\lambda t} \frac{(\lambda t)^n}{n!} \left[\frac{1}{t} \int_0^t H(x) \, dx \right]^n$$

$$= \exp \left\{ - \lambda \int_0^t [1 - H(x)] \, dx \right\}.$$

Furthermore, it is obvious that

$$m(t + \Delta t) - m(t) = \lambda P_0(t) \Delta t + o(\Delta t),$$

I

i.e. $m'(t) = \lambda P_0(t)$. Thus

$$\phi(s) = 1 - \frac{\lambda}{\lambda + s}\left[\lambda \int_0^\infty e^{-st-\lambda\int_0^t [1-H(x)]\,dx}\,dt\right]^{-1},$$

and $F(x)$ can be obtained by inversion. Hence we obtain that $\mu = -\phi'(0) = e^{\lambda\alpha}/\lambda$ is the mean value and

$$\sigma^2 = \phi''(0) - [\phi'(0)]^2 = \frac{2\mu - \lambda\mu^2}{\lambda} + 2\lambda\mu^2 \int_0^\infty \left[P_0(t) - \frac{1}{\lambda\mu}\right] dt$$

is the variance of $F(x)$.

15. The method of solution is similar to that of Problem 12, where in this case

$$F(x) = \lambda \int_0^x H(x - y)e^{-\lambda y}\,dy \qquad \text{if } x \geq 0.$$

Thus

$$\mu = \frac{1 + \lambda\alpha}{\lambda} \quad \text{and} \quad \sigma^2 = \frac{1 + \lambda^2\beta^2}{\lambda^2}$$

are the mean value and variance of $F(x)$ respectively.

16. Suppose the impulses are produced by the counter at times $\tau_1, \tau_2, \ldots, \tau_n, \ldots$ where

$$\mathbf{P}\{\tau_n - \tau_{n-1} \leq x\} = F(x), \quad (n = 2, 3, \ldots),$$

$$\mu = \int_0^\infty xF(x) \quad \text{and} \quad \sigma^2 = \int_0^\infty (x - \mu)^2\,dF(x).$$

Denote by $\tau_1', \tau_2', \ldots, \tau_n' \ldots$ the sequence of the instants of the recorded impulses, then the time differences $\tau'_n - \tau'_{n-1}(n = 2, 3, \ldots)$ are identically-distributed independent random variables but their distribution function $G(x)$ is not known at present. Let

$$A = \int_0^\infty x\,dG(x).$$

The density of recorded impulses is $f' = 1/A$. If we introduce

$$m(t) = \sum_{n=1}^\infty F_n(t),$$

the expectation of the number of impulses occurring in $(0, t]$, then by the theorem of the total probability we can write

$$G(x) = \begin{cases} 0 & \text{if } x < \tau, \\ \int_{\tau}^{x} [1 - F(x - u)]\, dm(u) & \text{if } x \geq \tau. \end{cases}$$

Hence

$$A = \mu[1 + m(\tau)].$$

17. The Laplace–Stieltjes transform of $F(x)$ in Problem 11 is

$$\phi(s) = \frac{\lambda e^{-\alpha(\lambda + s)}}{s + \lambda e^{-\alpha(\lambda + s)}}$$

and since

$$\int_{0}^{\infty} e^{-st}\, dm(t) = \frac{\phi(s)}{1 - \phi(s)},$$

therefore

$$m(t) = \begin{cases} 0 & \text{if } t < \alpha, \\ \lambda e^{-\lambda \alpha}(t - \alpha) & \text{if } t \geq \alpha, \end{cases}$$

and $\mu = e^{\lambda \alpha}/\lambda$. Hence

$$f' = \begin{cases} \dfrac{\lambda e^{-\lambda \alpha}}{1 + \lambda e^{-\lambda \alpha}(\tau - \alpha)} & \text{if } \tau > \alpha, \\ \lambda e^{-\lambda \alpha} & \text{if } \tau \leq \alpha. \end{cases}$$

18. The Laplace–Stieltjes transform of $F(x)$ in Problem 12 is

$$\psi(s) = \frac{\lambda e^{-s\alpha}}{\lambda + s}$$

and since

$$\int_{0}^{\infty} e^{-st}\, dm(t) = \frac{\phi(s)}{1 - \phi(s)},$$

therefore

$$m(t) = \sum_{k=0}^{[t/\alpha]} \left[1 - \sum_{j=0}^{k} e^{-\lambda(t - k\alpha)} \frac{\lambda^j (t - k\alpha)^j}{j!} \right] \quad \text{and} \quad \mu = \frac{1 + \lambda \alpha}{\lambda}.$$

Hence

$$f' = \frac{\lambda}{(1 + \lambda \alpha)[1 + m(\tau)]}.$$

19. Assume for the sake of simplicity that the system is in state E_m at time $t = 0$. Let the transitions $E_{m-1} \rightarrow E_m$ occur at the instants $\tau_1, \tau_2, \ldots, \tau_n, \ldots$ In this case the time differences $\tau_n - \tau_{n-1}$ ($n = 1, 2, 3, \ldots; \tau_0 = 0$) are identically-distributed independent random variables with distribution function $F(x)$. Let μ and σ^2 be the mean value and variance of $F(x)$. It is true that the density of the m-fold chance coincidences is $f = 1/\mu$ and the number of m-fold chance coincidences occurring in the time interval $(0, t]$ has an asymptotically normal distribution, as $t \rightarrow \infty$, with mean value t/μ and variance $\sigma^2 t/\mu^3$. If $m(t)$ denotes the expected number of m-fold chance coincidences occurring in the time interval $(0, t]$ and

$$\phi(s) = \int_0^\infty e^{-sx}\, dF(x),$$

then

$$\phi(s) = \frac{\displaystyle\int_0^\infty e^{-st}\, dm(t)}{1 + \displaystyle\int_0^\infty e^{-st}\, dm(t)}.$$

In our case $m'(t) = m\lambda P(t)[1 - P(t)]^{m-1}$, where $P(t)$ is the probability that there is no impulse present in one selected tube. It is easy to see that $P(t)$ satisfies the differential equation

$$\alpha P'(t) + (1 + \lambda\alpha)P(t) = 1, \text{ where } P(0) = 0;$$

the solution is

$$P(t) = \frac{1}{1 + \lambda\alpha}\left(1 - e^{-\frac{1+\lambda\alpha}{\alpha}t}\right).$$

Thus

$$\phi(s) = 1 - \left\{1 + m\lambda \int_0^\infty [1 - P(t)]^{m-1}P(t)e^{-st}\, dt\right\}^{-1}$$

$$= 1 - \left\{1 + \frac{m\lambda\alpha}{(1 + \lambda\alpha)^m} \sum_{j=0}^{m-1} \binom{m-1}{j}\right.$$

$$\left. \cdot \left[\frac{(\lambda\alpha)^{m-1-j}}{s\alpha + j(1 + \lambda\alpha)} - \frac{(\lambda\alpha)^{m-1-j}}{s\alpha + (j+1)(1 + \lambda\alpha)}\right]\right\}^{-1},$$

hence

$$\mu = \frac{(1 + \lambda\alpha)^m}{m\lambda^m\alpha^{m-1}}$$

and

$$\sigma^2 = \frac{(1+\lambda\alpha)^{m-1}\left\{(1+\lambda\alpha)^{m+1}+2\left[\sum_{j=1}^{m-1}\binom{m}{j+1}\frac{(\lambda\alpha)^{m-j}}{j} - m(\lambda\alpha)^m\right]\right\}}{m^2\lambda^{2m}\alpha^{2m-2}}.$$

20. Let $\tau_1, \tau_2, \ldots, \tau_n, \ldots$ denote the instants when impulses appear. Write $\mathbf{P}\{\tau_n - \tau_{n-1} \leq x\} = F(x)$ if $n = 1, 2, 3, \ldots$ $(\tau_0 = 0)$ and let μ and σ^2 be the mean value and variance of $F(x)$. If $\tau_1', \tau_2', \ldots,$ $\tau', \ldots$ is the sequence of the instants of registration, then $\{\tau_n'\}$ is a sequence of recurrent events. Let $G(x)$ be the common distribution function of the random variables $\tau_n' - \tau_{n-1}'$ and let A be its mean value and B^2 its variance. Since $\tau_1' = \tau_1 + \tau_2 + \ldots + \tau_{\nu_1}$, therefore $\mathbf{E}\{\tau_1'\} = \mathbf{E}\{\nu_1\}\mathbf{E}\{\tau_1\}$ and $\mathbf{D}^2\{\tau_1'\} = \mathbf{E}^2\{\tau_1\}\mathbf{D}^2\{\nu_1\} + \mathbf{D}^2\{\tau_1\}\mathbf{E}\{\nu_1\}$, which shows that $A = a\mu$ and $B^2 = \mu^2 b^2 + \sigma^2 a$. The number of registrations in the time interval $(0, t]$ is asymptotically normal if $t \to \infty$, with mean value t/A and variance $B^2 t/A^3$.

21. In this case the density function $f(x) = F'(x)$ exists, and by inverting (26) we obtain

$$f(x) = \frac{1}{2\pi}\frac{a}{a^2 + x^2}.$$

22. Let $\eta_t = (\xi_t - \mathbf{E}\{\xi_t\})/\mathbf{D}\{\xi_t\}$, then

$$
\begin{aligned}
|R(t + \Delta t) - R(t)| &= |\mathbf{E}\{\eta_{t+\Delta t}\eta_0\} - \mathbf{E}\{\eta\,\eta_0\}| \\
&= |\mathbf{E}\{(\eta_{t+\Delta t} - \eta_t)\eta_0\}| \\
&\leq \sqrt{\mathbf{E}\{(\eta_{t+\Delta t} - \eta_t)^2\}\mathbf{E}\{\eta_0{}^2\}} \\
&= \sqrt{\mathbf{E}\{(\eta_{t+\Delta t} - \eta_t)^2\}} \\
&= \sqrt{2[1 - R(\Delta t)]} \to 0 \qquad \text{if} \quad \Delta t \to 0.
\end{aligned}
$$

23. At present $\mathbf{E}\{\xi_t\} = 0$, $\mathbf{E}\{\xi_t^2\} = 1$ and $R(t) = \cos\alpha t$. We find from (26) that

$$F(x) = \begin{cases} 0 & \text{if} \quad x \leq -\alpha, \\ \frac{1}{2} & \text{if} \quad -\alpha < x \leq \alpha, \\ 1 & \text{if} \quad x > \alpha. \end{cases}$$

24. The spectral density function of the process $\{\xi_t\}$ is

$$f(\lambda) = \frac{1}{2\pi} \frac{a}{a^2 + \lambda^2} = \frac{a}{2\pi} \frac{1}{(\lambda + ia)(\lambda - ia)}.$$

Consider the function

$$\Psi_\tau(\lambda) = \frac{a}{2\pi} \frac{e^{i\tau\lambda} - \Phi_\tau(\lambda)}{(\lambda + ia)(\lambda - ia)}.$$

This must be regular on the upper half-plane, therefore,

$$\Phi_\tau(ia) = e^{-a\tau}.$$

On the other hand, since $\Phi_\tau(\lambda)$ must be regular on the lower half-plane, therefore $\Phi_\tau(\lambda)$ can have a singularity only at $\lambda = \infty$. It follows from the requirement concerning $|\lambda| \longrightarrow \infty$ that $\Phi_\tau(\lambda)$ is a constant, i.e. $\Phi_\tau(\lambda) = e^{-a\tau}$. Hence $L_\tau(t) = e^{-a\tau}\xi(t)$ or $\xi(t + \tau) \sim e^{-a\tau}\xi(t)$. The mean-square error of the prediction is

$$\sigma_\tau^2 = (1 - e^{-2a\tau}).$$

25. The correlation function of the process $\{\xi_t\}$ is

$$R(\tau) = \frac{C}{2^{3/2}\alpha^{1/2}} e^{-\frac{\alpha\tau}{\sqrt{2}}}\Big(\cos \frac{\alpha\tau}{\sqrt{2}} + \sin \frac{\alpha\tau}{\sqrt{2}}\Big)$$

and the requirement $R(0) = 1$ shows that $C = 2^{3/2}\alpha^{1/2}$.

By the conditions 1°, 2°, 3° of Section 2 it can be shown that $\Phi_\tau(\lambda) = A\lambda + B$, and the coefficients A and B are easy to determine. Thus

$$\Phi_\tau(\lambda) = \frac{\sqrt{2} e^{-\frac{\alpha\tau}{\sqrt{2}}}}{\alpha}\Big(\sin \frac{\alpha\tau}{\sqrt{2}}\Big)i\lambda + e^{-\frac{\alpha\tau}{\sqrt{2}}}\Big(\cos \frac{\alpha\tau}{\sqrt{2}} + \sin \frac{\alpha\tau}{\sqrt{2}}\Big),$$

whence

$$L_\tau(t) = \frac{\sqrt{2} e^{-\frac{\alpha\tau}{\sqrt{2}}}}{\alpha}\Big(\sin \frac{\alpha\tau}{\sqrt{2}}\Big)\xi'(t) + e^{-\frac{\alpha\tau}{\sqrt{2}}}\Big(\cos \frac{\alpha\tau}{\sqrt{2}} + \sin \frac{\alpha\tau}{\sqrt{2}}\Big)\xi(t)$$

and $\xi(t + \tau) \sim L_\tau(t)$. The mean-square error of the linear predictions is

$$\sigma_\tau^2 = \frac{C}{2\alpha^3\sqrt{2}}\Big[1 - 2e^{-\alpha\tau\sqrt{2}} - \sqrt{2} e^{-\alpha\tau\sqrt{2}}\sin\Big(\alpha\tau\sqrt{2} - \frac{\pi}{4}\Big)\Big].$$

26. According to conditions 1°, 2°, 3° of Section 2 we have $\Phi_\tau(\lambda) = (A\lambda + iB)/(\lambda - i\alpha)$, where

$$A = e^{-\frac{\alpha\tau}{\sqrt{2}}} \left[\cos \frac{\alpha\tau}{\sqrt{2}} + (\sqrt{2} - 1) \sin \frac{\alpha\tau}{\sqrt{2}}\right],$$

$$B = \alpha e^{-\frac{\alpha\tau}{\sqrt{2}}} \left[\cos \frac{\alpha\tau}{\sqrt{2}} - (\sqrt{2} - 1) \sin \frac{\alpha\tau}{\sqrt{2}}\right].$$

Consequently

$$L_\tau(t) = A \int_{-\infty}^{\infty} e^{i\lambda t} \, d\zeta(\lambda) - (\alpha A - B) \int_{-\infty}^{\infty} \frac{e^{i\lambda t}}{\alpha + i\lambda} \, d\zeta(\lambda),$$

or

$$L_\tau(t) = A\xi(t) - (\alpha A - B) \int_0^{\infty} e^{-\alpha s} \xi(t - s) \, ds,$$

and $\xi(t + \tau) \sim L_\tau(t)$. The mean-square error of the linear prediction is

$$\sigma^2 = \frac{C}{\sqrt{2}\alpha} [1 - (\sqrt{2} - 1)e^{-\alpha\tau\sqrt{2}} (\sqrt{2} + \cos \alpha\tau\sqrt{2})].$$

27. Denote by ξ_t the number of electrons emitted in the time interval $(0, t]$ and let η_t be the value of the anode-current at the instant t. Then

$$\eta_t = \sum_{0 \leq \tau_k \leq t} f(t - \tau_k, \chi_k),$$

where the sequence $\{\tau_k\}$ denotes the time instants at which electron emission takes place, and χ_k is the initial velocity of the electron emitted at τ_k. The random variables $\{\chi_k\}$ are identically-distributed independent random variables with distribution function $H(x)$. (If we suppose that the Maxwell–Boltzmann statistic is valid for the electrons, then

$$H(x) = 1 - e^{-\frac{mx^2}{2kT}}, \qquad (x \geq 0),$$

where $m = 9 \cdot 11 . 10^{-28}$ gr is the electron-mass, $k = 1 \cdot 38 . 10^{-16}$ erg/ grad is Boltzmann's constant and T is the absolute temperature of the cathode.) Let

$$\Phi(t, z) = \mathbf{E}\{e^{i\eta_t z}\}, \quad \phi(t, z) = \int_0^\infty e^{izf(t, x)} \, dH(x).$$

By the theorem of total expectation we can write

$$\mathbf{E}\{e^{iz\eta_t}\} = \sum_{n=0}^\infty \mathbf{P}\{\xi_t = n\}\mathbf{E}\{e^{iz\eta_t} \mid \xi_t = n\}.$$

Here $\mathbf{E}\{e^{iz\eta_t} \mid \xi_t = 0\} = 1$ and it follows from a well-known property of the Poisson distribution (Problem 7, Chapter 2) that

$$\mathbf{E}\{e^{iz\eta_t} \mid \xi_t = 1\} = \frac{1}{t} \int_0^t \phi(u, z) \, du,$$

and

$$\mathbf{E}\{e^{iz\eta_t} \mid \xi_t = n\} = [\mathbf{E}\{e^{iz\eta_t} \mid \xi_t = 1\}]^n.$$

Thus

$$\Phi(t, z) = \exp\left\{-\lambda \int_0^t [1 - \phi(u, z)] \, du\right\}.$$

Hence

$$\mathbf{E}\{\eta_t\} = -i\left(\frac{d \log \Phi(t, z)}{dz}\right)_{z=0} = \lambda \int_0^t \left[\int_0^\infty f(u, x) \, dH(x)\right] du$$

and

$$\mathbf{D}^2\{\eta_t\} = \left(\frac{d^2 \log \Phi(t, z)}{dz^2}\right)_{z=0} = \lambda \int_0^t \left[\int_0^\infty (f(u, x))^2 \, dH(x)\right] du.$$

If we suppose that

$$\int_0^\infty \left[\int_0^\infty |f(u, x)| \, dH(x)\right] du < \infty,$$

then it can be shown, using a well-known theorem of *Lévy* and *Cramér* concerning the convergence of characteristic functions, that the limiting distribution $\lim_{t \to \infty} F(t, x) = F(x)$ exists and that $\Phi(z) = \lim_{\to \infty} \Phi(t, z)$ is the characteristic function of $F(x)$. In this case we can define the stationary process $\{\eta_t^*\}$ for which

$$\mathbf{E}\{e^{iz\eta_t^*}\} = \Phi(z) = \exp\left\{-\lambda \int_0^\infty [1 - \phi(u, z)]\, du\right\}.$$

$F(x)$ can be determined by inversion. We have

$$\mathbf{E}\{\eta_t^*\} = \lambda \int_0^\infty \left[\int_0^\infty f(u, x)\, dH(x)\right]$$

and

$$\mathbf{D}^2\{\eta_t^*\} = \lambda \int_0^\infty \left[\int_0^\infty (f(u, x))^2\, dH(x)\right] du,$$

if it exists.

28. Let $R(\tau) = \mathbf{R}\{\eta_{t-\tau}^*, \eta_t^*\}$. In order to determine $R(\tau)$ let us define a new process $\Theta_t^* = \eta_t^* + \eta_{t-\tau}$. This is again a stationary process and it differs from η_t^* only in that now $g(u, x) = f(u, x) + f(u - \tau, x)$ describes the intensity of a current impulse starting at $u = 0$ instead of $f(u, x)$. According to Problem 27 we obtain

$$\mathbf{D}^2\{\Theta_t^*\} = \lambda \int_0^\infty \left[\int_0^\infty (f(u, x) + f(u - \tau, x))^2\, dH(x)\right] du.$$

On the other hand, since $\Theta_t^* = \eta_t^* + \eta_{t-\tau}^*$ we have

$$\mathbf{D}^2\{\Theta_t^*\} = 2\mathbf{D}^2\{\eta_t^*\}[1 + R(\tau)].$$

By comparing these formulae we obtain

$$R(\tau) = \frac{\displaystyle\int_0^\infty \left[\int_0^\infty f(u, x)f(u - \tau, x)\, dH(x)\right] du}{\displaystyle\int_0^\infty \left[\int_0^\infty (f(u, x))^2\, dH(x)\right] du}.$$

Now according to (26) it is true for the spectral distribution function $F(\omega)$ that

$$F'(\omega) = \frac{2\pi\lambda}{\sigma^2} \int_0^\infty |A(\omega, x)|^2\, dH(x),$$

where

$$A(\omega, x) = \frac{1}{2\pi} \int_0^\infty f(u, x)e^{-i\omega u}\, du, \qquad \sigma^2 = \mathbf{D}^2\{\eta_t^*\}.$$

In physics we understand by the *spectral function* of the process $\{\eta_t^*\}$ the function

$$G(\nu) = m^2 + \sigma^2[F(2\pi\nu) - F(-2\pi\nu)],$$

where $m = \mathbf{E}\{\eta_t^*\}$. For, if the current η_t^* is passed through a unit resistance, then the dissipated average power is

$$\lim_{T \to \infty} \mathbf{E}\left\{\frac{1}{2T} \int_{-T}^T \eta_t^{*2}\, dt\right\} = \mathbf{E}\{\eta_t^{*2}\} = m^2 + \sigma^2$$

and $G(\nu)$ furnishes the frequency distribution of this power over the frequency range $0 \le \nu < \infty$, i.e. $G(\nu)$ is the average power produced by the components of the current the frequency of which is contained in the interval $(0, \nu)$. Now $G(0) = m^2$ and

$$G'(\nu) = 8\pi^2\lambda^2 \int_0^\infty |A(2\pi\nu, x)|^2\, dH(x),$$

for $0 < \nu < \infty$.

29. By formulae (27) and (28) we have

$$\mathbf{E}\left\{\frac{1}{T} \int_0^T \eta_t^*\, dt\right\} = \mathbf{E}\{\eta_t^*\} = m$$

and

$$\mathbf{D}^2\left\{\frac{1}{T} \int_0^T \eta_t^*\, dt\right\} = \frac{\sigma^2}{T^2} \int_0^T \int_0^T R(u - v)\, du\, dv$$
$$= \frac{2\sigma^2}{T^2} \int_0^T (T - \tau)R(\tau)\, d\tau.$$

30. Let d be the distance between the plates of the plane diode and let U be the anode potential. Now $H(x) = 1 \ (x \ge 0)$. Let the current impulse induced by an electron emitted at time $u = 0$ be $f(u, 0) = f(u)$ at the instant u. This function has the following form

$$f(u) = \begin{cases} 2\varepsilon u/\tau_0^2 & \text{if} \quad 0 \le u \le \tau_0, \\ 0 & \text{otherwise,} \end{cases}$$

where $\varepsilon = 1\cdot6.10^{-19}$ *coul.* is the electron charge and

$$\tau_0 = 2d/\sqrt{2\varepsilon U/m}$$

is the transit time of the electron. In this case

$$\mathbf{E}\{e^{iz\eta_t^*}\} = \Phi(z) = e^{-\lambda\tau_0} \exp\left\{\frac{\lambda\tau_0^2}{2iz\varepsilon}\left(e^{\frac{2iz\varepsilon}{\tau_0}} - 1\right)\right\},$$

whence

$$\mathbf{P}\{\eta_t^* \leq x\} = F(x) = e^{-\lambda\tau_0} + \frac{e^{-\lambda\tau_0\tau_0}}{2\varepsilon}$$

$$\cdot \int_0^{x\,[\frac{1}{2}y\tau_0/\varepsilon]} \sum_{j=0} (-1)^j \frac{(\lambda\tau_0)^j}{j!} \frac{I_{j-1}\left(2\sqrt{\lambda\tau_0\left(\frac{y\tau_0}{2\varepsilon} - j\right)}\right)}{\left(\sqrt{\lambda\tau_0\left(\frac{y\tau_0}{2\varepsilon} - j\right)}\right)^{j-1}} dy,$$

where

$$I_\rho(x) = \left(\frac{x}{2}\right)^\rho \sum_{\nu=0}^\infty \frac{(x/2)^{2\nu}}{\nu!\,\Gamma(\nu + \rho + 1)}$$

is the Bessel function of imaginary argument of order ρ. Now $\mathbf{E}\{\eta_t^*\} = \lambda/\varepsilon$. Let $\mathbf{E}\{\eta\} = I$, i.e. $\lambda = I/\varepsilon$, then

$$\mathbf{D}\{\eta_t^*\} = \sqrt{\frac{4\varepsilon I}{3\tau_0}}$$

and

$$R(\tau) = \begin{cases} 1 - \frac{3}{2}\frac{|\tau|}{\tau_0} + \frac{1}{2}\frac{|\tau|^3}{\tau_0^3} & \text{if } 0 \leq |\tau| \leq \tau_0, \\ 0 & \text{otherwise.} \end{cases}$$

We have for the spectral distribution function $G(\nu)$ that $G(0) = I^2$ and

$$G'(\nu) = 8\varepsilon I \frac{2(1 - \cos\Theta) + \Theta(\Theta - 2\sin\Theta)}{\Theta^4}$$

$$= 2\varepsilon I\left[1 - \frac{\Theta^2}{18} + \ldots\right] \quad \text{if } 0 < \nu < \infty,$$

where $\Theta = 2\pi\nu\tau_0$.

31. By applying the solution of Problem 29 we obtain

$$\mathbf{D}^2\left\{\frac{1}{T}\int_0^T \eta_t^* \, dt\right\} = \begin{cases} \dfrac{4\varepsilon I}{3\tau_0}\left[1 - \dfrac{1}{2}\dfrac{T}{\tau_0} + \dfrac{1}{20}\left(\dfrac{T}{\tau_0}\right)^3\right] & \text{if } 0 \leqq T \leqq \tau_0, \\[3ex] \dfrac{4\varepsilon I}{3\tau_0}\left[\dfrac{3}{4}\dfrac{\tau_0}{T} - \dfrac{1}{5}\left(\dfrac{\tau_0}{T}\right)^2\right] & \text{if } \tau_0 \leqq T < \infty. \end{cases}$$

32. We can write

$$\xi_t = \sum_{0 \leqq \tau_n \leqq t} \chi_n \, e^{-\alpha(t-\tau_n)},$$

where $\{\tau_n\}$ denotes the occurrence points of the events in the Poisson process, and the amplitudes χ_n are identically-distributed independent random variables with distribution function $H(x)$. Let

$$\Phi(t, z) = \mathbf{E}\{e^{iz\xi_t}\}, \quad \psi(z) = \int_0^\infty e^{izx} \, dH(x).$$

Denote by ν_t the number of events occurring in the Poisson process in the time interval $(0, t]$. By the theorem of the total expectation we can write

$$\mathbf{E}\{e^{iz\xi_t}\} = \sum_{n=0}^\infty \mathbf{P}\{\nu_t = n\}\mathbf{E}\{e^{iz\xi_t} \mid \nu_t = n\}.$$

Now $\mathbf{P}\{\nu_t = n\} = e^{-\lambda t}(\lambda t)^n/n!$, $\mathbf{E}\{e^{iz\xi_t} \mid \nu_t = 0\} = 1$ and the well-known property of Poisson processes (Problem 7 of Chapter 2) implies that

$$\mathbf{E}\{e^{iz\xi_t} \mid \nu_t = n\} = [\mathbf{E}\{e^{iz\xi_t} \mid \nu_t = 1\}]^n$$

and

$$\mathbf{E}\{e^{iz\xi_t} \mid \nu_t = 1\} = \frac{1}{t}\int_0^t \psi(ze^{-\alpha u}) \, du.$$

Thus finally

$$\Phi(t, z) = \exp\left\{-\lambda \int_0^t [1 - \psi(ze^{-\alpha u})] \, du\right\}.$$

We saw (Problem 31, Chapter 2) that if $\int_0^\infty x \, dH(x) < \alpha$, then

$\lim_{t \to \infty} \mathbf{P}\{\xi_t \le x\} = F(x)$ exists and the characteristic function of $F(x)$ is

$$\Phi(z) = \exp\left\{ -\frac{\lambda}{\alpha} \int_0^1 \frac{1 - \psi(zx)}{x} \, dx \right\}.$$

In the stationary case denote by $f(a)$ the density of registrations for a threshold potential a. Since the probability of a registration occurring during $(t, t + \Delta t)$ is

$$\lambda \Delta t \int_0^a [1 - H(a - x)] \, dF(x) + o(\Delta t),$$

therefore

$$f(a) = \lambda\left[F(a) - \int_0^a H(a - x) \, dF(x) \right].$$

If in particular the amplitudes of the potential impulses are constant μ, then

$$\Phi(z) = \frac{1}{(-iz\mu\gamma)^{\lambda/\alpha}} \exp\left\{ -\frac{\lambda}{\alpha} \int_\mu^\infty \frac{e^{izu}}{u} \, du \right\},$$

where $\gamma = e^c = 1 \cdot 781072 \ldots$, ($C = 0 \cdot 577215 \ldots$ is Euler's constant.) Hence

$$F(x) = \frac{1}{\Gamma\left(1 + \frac{\lambda}{\alpha}\right)(\mu\gamma)^{\lambda/\alpha}} \left[x^{\lambda/\alpha} + \sum_{n=1}^\infty \frac{(-1)^n(\lambda/\alpha)^n}{n!} \int_{n\mu}^x (x - y)^{\lambda/\alpha} f_n(y) \, dy \right],$$

where

$$f_1(x) = \begin{cases} 0 & \text{if } x < \mu, \\ \dfrac{1}{x} & \text{if } x \ge \mu, \end{cases}$$

and $f_n(x)$ is the n-th iterated convolution of $f_1(x)$ with itself. Now the density of registrations for the threshold potential a is

$$f(a) = \lambda[F(a) - F(a - \mu)].$$

33. Let $$\gamma = \int_0^\infty x \, dG(x).$$

In case (a) $\gamma = 1/\lambda$ and in case (b) $\gamma = (1 + \lambda\tau)/\lambda$. If $G(x)$ is not a lattice distribution, then the density of impulses is $1/\gamma$. However, an impulse is registered if and only if the voltage on the input resistance is less than a at the arrival point of the impulse but at this moment rises above a. The probability of this event is

$$\int_0^a [1 - H(a - x)] \, dP(x).$$

Consequently the density of registrations in the case of a threshold potential a is

$$f(a) = \frac{1}{\gamma} \left[P(a) - \int_0^a H(a - x) \, dP(x) \right].$$

REFERENCES

―

BOOKS

N. ARLEY: *On the Theory of Stochastic Processes and their Application to the Theory of Cosmic Radiation.* John Wiley and Sons, New York, 1943

M. S. BARTLETT: *An Introduction to Stochastic Processes.* University Press, Cambridge, 1955

A. BLANC-LAPIERRE et R. FORTET: *Théorie des Fonctions Aléatoires.* Masson et Cie, Paris, 1953

J. L. DOOB: *Stochastic Processes.* John Wiley and Sons, New York, 1953

W. FELLER: *An Introduction to Probability Theory and its Applications.* John Wiley and Sons, New York, 1950; Second edition 1957

A. KHINTCHINE: *Asymptotische Gesetze der Wahrscheinlichkeitsrechnung.* Julius Springer, Berlin, 1933; Chelsea, New York, 1948

A. KOLMOGOROFF: *Grundbegriffe der Wahrscheinlichkeitsrechnung.* Julius Springer, Berlin, 1933; Chelsea, New York, 1948

A. N. KOLMOGOROV: *Foundations of the Theory of Probability.* Chelsea, New York, 1950

P. LÉVY: *Processes Stochastiques et Mouvement Brownien.* Gauthier-Villars, Paris, 1948

В. И. РОМАНОВСКИЙ: *Дискретные цели Маркова.* Москва, 1949

Т. А. САРЫМСАКОВ: *Основы теории процессов Маркова.* Москва, 1954

PAPERS

INTRODUCTION

1. BACHELIER: *Calcul des Probabilités.* Gauthier-Villars, Paris, 1912

A. EINSTEIN: *Investigations on the Theory of the Brownian Movement.* Dover Publications, 1956

A. K. ERLANG: 'Solution of some problems in the theory of probabilities of significance in automatic telephone exchanges'. *Post Office Electrical Engineers' Journal* **10**, 1918, 189–97

W. SCHOTTKY: 'Über spontane Stromschwankungen in verschiedenen Elektrizitätsleitern'. *Annalen der Physik* **57**, 1918, 541–67

M. V. SMOLUCHOWSKI: 'Drei Vorträge über Diffusion, Brownsche Bewegung und Koagulation von Kolloidteilchen'. *Physik. Zeitschrift* **17**, 1916, 557 and 585

CHAPTER 1

A. A. ANIS: 'On the distribution of the range of partial sums of independent random variables'. *Proc. Math. and Phys. Soc. of Egypt* **1**, 1954, 83–9

W. FELLER: 'Fluctuation theory of recurrent events'. *Trans. Amer. Math. Soc.* **67**, 1949, 98–119

'The problem of *n* liars and Markov chains'. *American Mathematical Monthly* **58**, 1951, 606–8

F. G. FOSTER: 'On the stochastic matrices associated with certain queueing processes'. *Ann. Math. Stat.* **24**, 1953, 355–60

T. E. HARRIS: 'Some mathematical models for branching processes'. *Proc. Second Berkeley Symp. Math. Stat. and Prob.* 1951, pp. 305–27

A. M. ЯГЛОМ: «Введение в теорию стационарных случайных функции», *Успехи Матем. Наук* **7**, 1252, 3–168

M. KAC: 'Random walk and the theory of Brownian motion'. *American Mathematical Monthly* **54**, 1947, 369–91

D. G. KENDALL: 'Stochastic processes occurring in the theory of queues and their analysis by the method of the inbedded Markov chain'. *Ann. Math. Stat.* **24**, 1953, 338–54

A. KOLMOGOROFF: 'Zur Theorie der Markoffschen Ketten'. *Math. Annalen* **112**, 1935–6, 155–60

A. Н. КОЛМОГОРОВ: «Цели Маркова со счётным числом возможных состояний». *М. Бюлл. Ун-та, А* **I:3**, 1937, 1–16

D. V. LINDLEY: 'The theory of queues with a single server'. *Proc. Cambridge Phil. Soc.* **48**, 1952, 277–89

A. RÉNYI: 'Dimensionnement rationnel des compresseurs et des réservoirs d'air pour fournir aux usines l'air comprimé'. *Publ. de l'Inst. Math. Appl. de l'Acad. Sci. Hong.* **1**, 1952, 105–38

L. TAKÁCS: 'On stochastic processes connected with certain physical recording apparatuses'. *Acta Math. Acad. Sci. Hung.* **6**, 1955, 363–80

'On the generalization of Erlang's formula'. *Acta Math. Acad. Sci. Hung.* **7**, 1956, 419–33

CHAPTER 2

W. FELLER: 'Zur Theorie der stochastischen Prozesse'. *Math. Annalen* **113**, 1936, 113–60

'On the integrodifferential equations of purely discontinuous Markoff processes'. *Trans. Amer. Math. Soc.* **48**, 1940, 488–511

'On the theory of stochastic processes with particular reference to applications'. *Proc. First Berkeley Symp. Math. Stat. and Prob.* 1949, pp. 403–32

L. JÁNOSSY, A. RÉNYI and J. ACZÉL: 'On composed Poisson distributions, I'. *Acta Math. Acad. Sci. Hung.* **1**, 1950, 209–34

A. KOLMOGOROFF: 'Über die analytischen Methoden in der Wahrscheinlichkeitsrechnung'. *Math. Annalen* **104**, 1931, 415–58

L. TAKÁCS: 'On secondary processes generated by a Poisson process and their applications in physics'. *Acta Math. Acad. Sci. Hung.* **5**, 1954, 203–36

'Investigation of waiting time problems by reduction to Markov processes.' *Acta Math. Acad. Sci. Hung.* **6**, 1955, 101–29

'On some probabilistic problems in the theory of nuclear reactors.' *Publ. Math. Inst. Hung. Acad. of Sci.* **1**, 1956, 55–66.

'On secondary stochastic processes generated by a multidimensional Poisson process.' *Publ. Math. Inst. Hung. Acad. of Sci.* **2**, 1957, 71–80

'On a general probability theorem and its applications in the theory of stochastic processes.' *Proc. Cambridge Phil. Soc.* **54**, 1958, 219–24

J. M. WHITTAKER: 'The shot effect for showers.' *Proc. Cambridge Phil. Soc.* **33**, 1937, 451–8

CHAPTER 3

D. BLACKWELL: 'A renewal theorem'. *Duke Math. Journ.* **15**, 1948 145–50

H. CRAMÉR: 'On the theory of stationary random processes'. *Annt Math. Stat.* **41**, 1940, 215–30

J. L. DOOB: 'Renewal theory from the point of view of the theory of probability'. *Trans. Amer. Math. Soc.* **63**, 1948, 422–38

'Time series and harmonic analysis.' *Proc. First Berkeley Symp. Math. Stat. and Prob.* 1949, pp. 303–43

W. FELLER: 'On the integral equation of renewal theory.' *Ann. Math. Stat.* **12**, 1944, 243–67

'On probability problems in the theory of counters.' *Couran. Anniversary Volume,* New York, 1948, pp. 105–15

A. M. ЯГЛОМ: «Введение в теорию стационарных случайных функции» *Успехи Матем. Наук* **7**, 1952, 3–168

A. KHINTCHINE: 'Korrelationstheorie der stationären stochastichen Prozesse'. *Math. Annalen* **19**, 1934, 604–10.

W. L. SMITH: 'Asymptotic renewal theorems'. *Proc. Roy. Soc Edinburgh, A* **64**, 1954, 9–48

'Renewal theory and its ramifications.' *Jour. Roy. Soc. B.* **20**, 1958, 243–84

L. TAKÁCS: 'A new method for discussing recurrent stochastic processes'. *Publ. de l'Inst. Math. Appl. de l'Acad. Sci. Hong.* **2**. 1953, 135–51

'On secondary processes generated by recurrent processes.' *Acta Math. Acad. Sci. Hung.* **7**, 1956, 17–29

'On stochastic processes in the theory of counters.' *Magy. Tud. Akad. Mat. és Fiz. Oszt. Közl.* **6**, 1956, 369–421

'On a probability problem arising in the theory of counters.' *Proc. Cambridge Phil. Soc.* **52**, 1956, 488–98

'On the sequence of events, selected by a counter from a recurrent process of events.' *Теория Вероятностей и ее Применения* **1**, 1956, 90–102

'Über die wahrscheinlichkeitstheoretische Behandlung der Anodenstromschwankungen von Elektronenröhren.' *Acta Phys. Acad. Sci. Hung.* **7**, 1957, 25–50

'On some probability problems concerning the theory of counters'. *Acta Math. Acad. Sci. Hung.* **8**, 1957, 127–138

S. TÄCKLIND: 'Elementare Behandlung vom Erneuerungsproblem'. *Skand. Aktuar.* **27**, 1944, pp. 1–15

'Fourier-analytische Behandlung vom Erneuerungsproblem'. *Skand. Aktuar,* **28**, 1945, pp. 68–105

INDEX